PIGLING

A CINDERELLA STORY

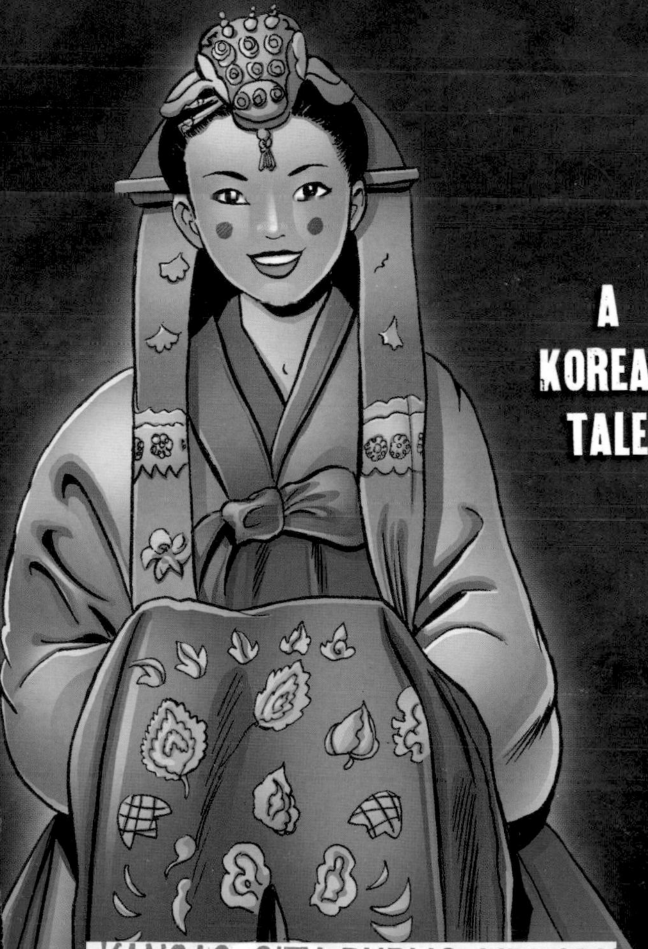

A
KOREAN
TALE

GRAPHIC UNIVERSE™

STORY BY
DAN JOLLEY

PENCILS AND INKS BY
ANNE TIMMONS

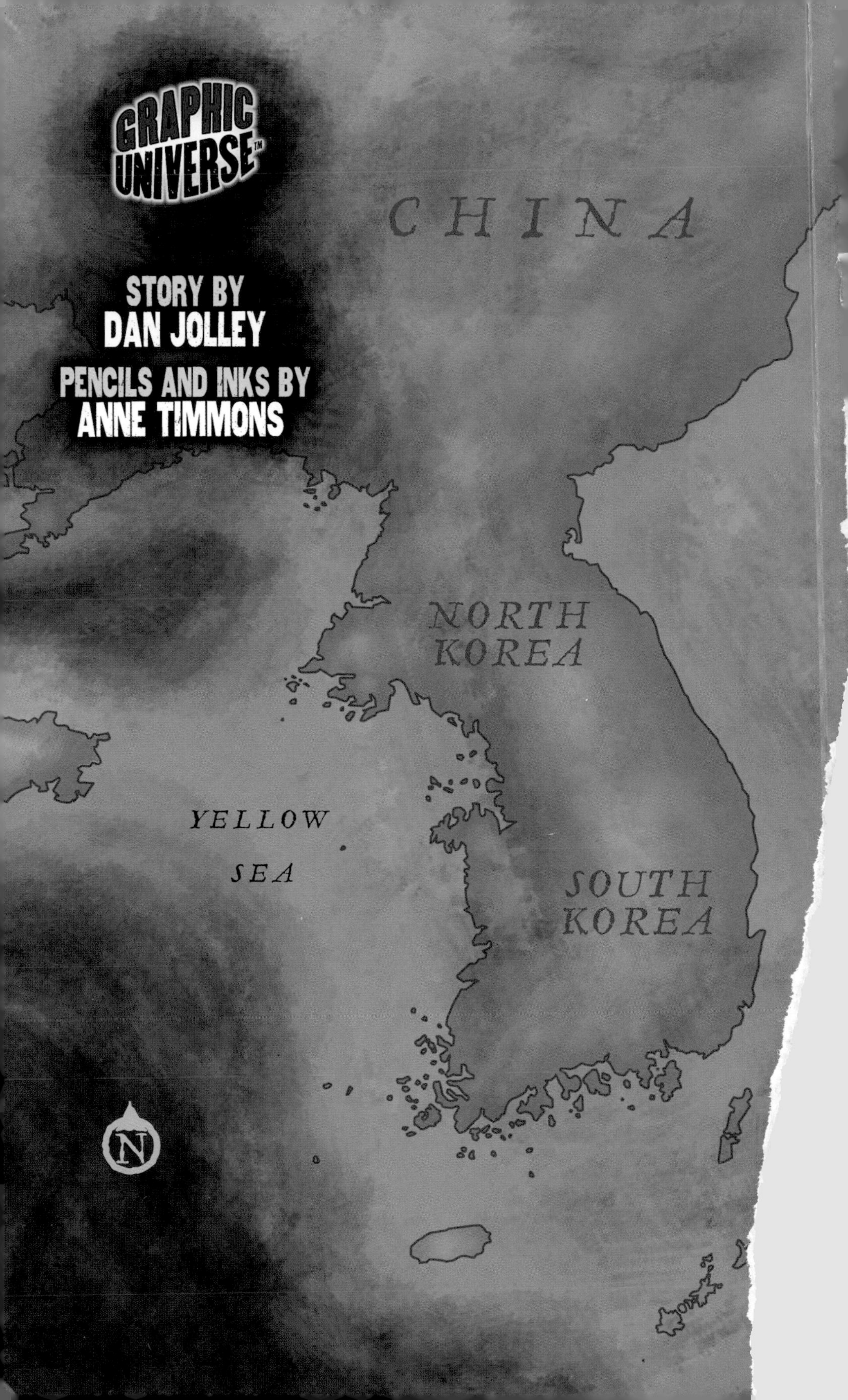
CHINA
NORTH KOREA
YELLOW SEA
SOUTH KOREA
N

PIGLING

A CINDERELLA STORY

A KOREAN TALE

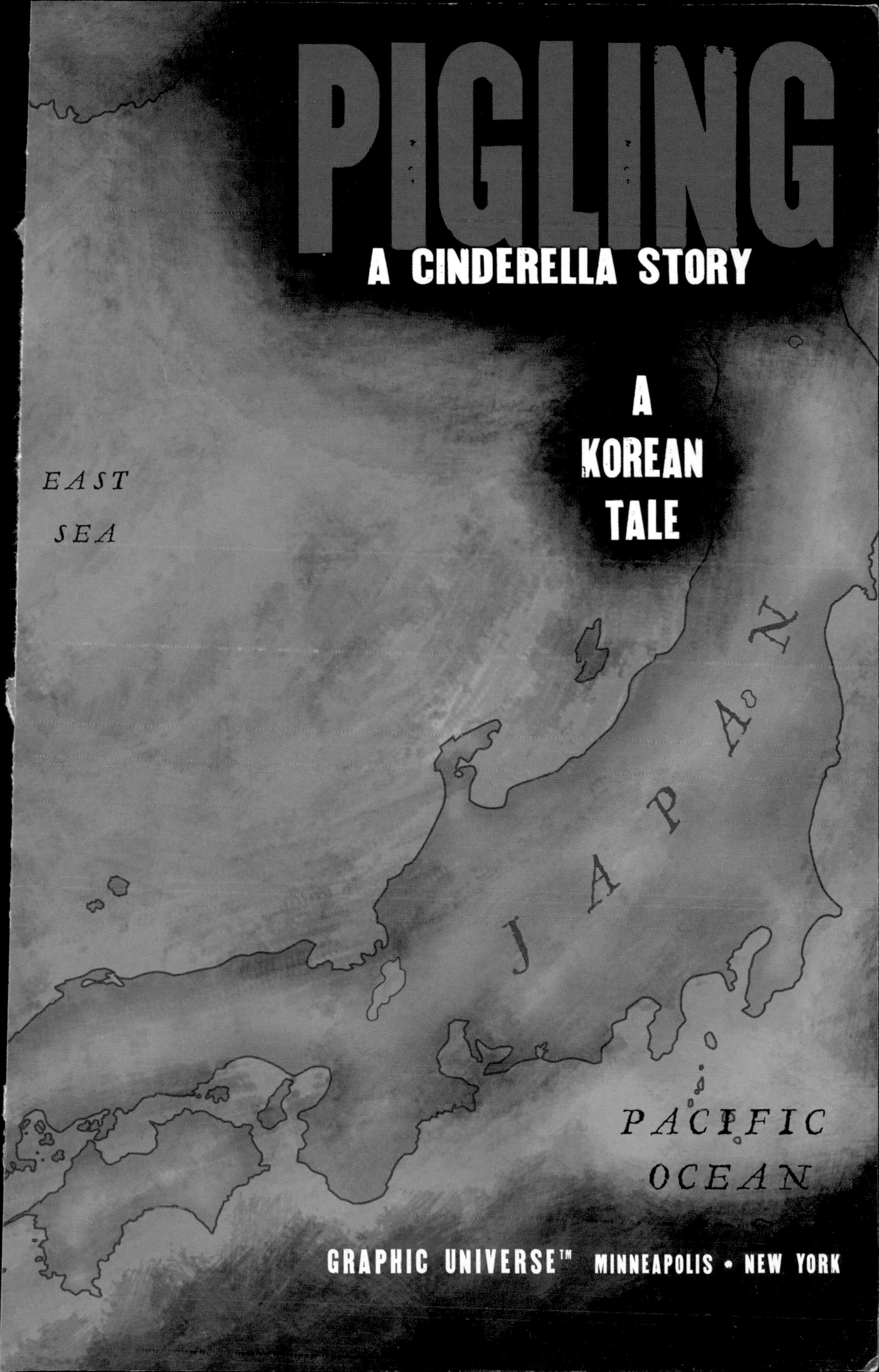
EAST SEA
JAPAN
PACIFIC OCEAN

GRAPHIC UNIVERSE™ MINNEAPOLIS • NEW YORK

PIGLING IS A KOREAN CINDERELLA STORY. IT HAS BEEN
TOLD THROUGHOUT KOREA FOR CENTURIES. MANY
DIFFERENT VERSIONS OF THE STORY EXIST, BUT THEY ALL
TELL OF A YOUNG GIRL WHO SUFFERS AT THE HANDS OF A
WICKED STEPMOTHER. THE STORIES ALSO FEATURE A
HELPFUL GOBLIN THAT REVEALS ITSELF IN THE FORM OF
FRIENDLY FOREST CREATURES. THESE CREATURES STEP
FORWARD TO ASSIST THE HEROINE WHENEVER SHE NEEDS A
HELPING HAND.

IN CREATING THIS ADAPTATION OF PIGLING, AUTHOR
DAN JOLLEY RELIED ON SEVERAL TELLINGS OF THE TALE,
INCLUDING WILLIAM ELLIOT GRIFFIS'S PIGLING AND HER
PROUD SISTER AS IT APPEARS IN OLIVE BEAUPRÉ
MILLER'S THROUGH FAIRY HALLS. JOLLEY ALSO WORKED
WITH CONSULTANT MINSOOK KIM, PH.D., OF THE
UNIVERSITY OF CALIFORNIA, BERKELEY, TO ENSURE THAT
THE STORY'S DETAILS ARE HISTORICALLY ACCURATE. ARTIST
ANNE TIMMONS REFERRED TO NUMEROUS HISTORICAL
SOURCES AND WORKED CLOSELY WITH KIM TO BRING THE
STORY'S DYNAMIC IMAGERY TO LIFE.

STORY BY DAN JOLLEY

PENCILS AND INKS BY ANNE TIMMONS

COLORING BY HI-FI DESIGN

LETTERING BY MARSHALL DILLON AND
TERRI DELGADO

CONSULTANT: MINSOOK KIM, PH.D.,
UNIVERSITY OF CALIFORNIA, BERKELEY

Copyright © 2009 by Lerner Publishing Group, Inc.

Graphic Universe™ is a trademark of Lerner
Publishing Group, Inc.

Graphic Universe™
A division of Lerner Publishing Group, Inc.
241 First Avenue North
Minneapolis, MN 55401 U.S.A.

Website address: www.lernerbooks.com

Library of Congress Cataloging-in-Publication Data

Jolley, Dan.
     Pigling : a Cinderella story : a Korean tale / story
by Dan Jolley ; pencils and inks by Anne Timmons.
     p. cm. — (Graphic myths and legends)
     Includes index.
     ISBN 978-0-8225-7174-2 (lib. bdg. : alk. paper)
     1. Graphic novels. I. Timmons, Anne. II. Title.
III. Title: Cinderella story: a Korean tale.
PN6727.J58P55 2008
741.5'973—dc22   2007040891

Manufactured in the United States of America
2 3 4 5 6 7 - DP - 14 13 12 11 10 09

TABLE OF CONTENTS

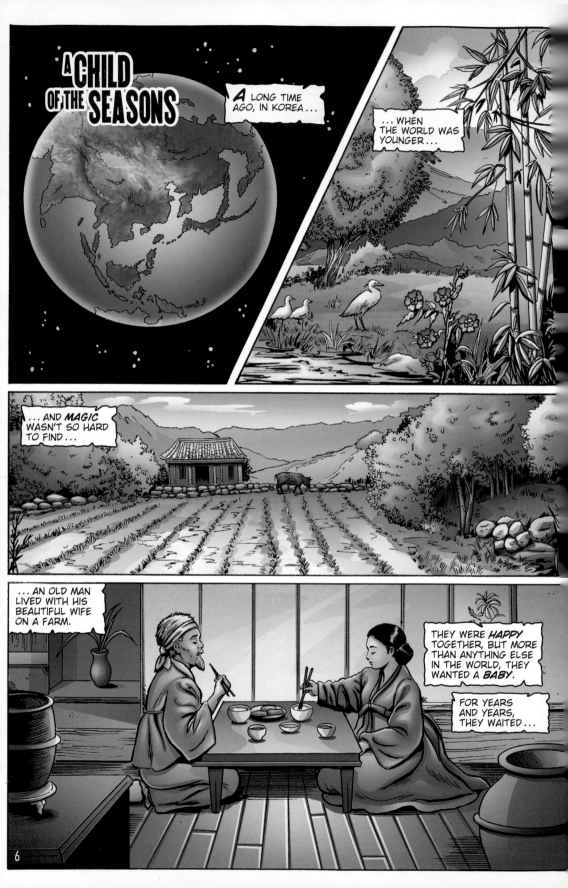

A CHILD OF THE SEASONS

A LONG TIME AGO, IN KOREA...

... WHEN THE WORLD WAS YOUNGER...

... AND *MAGIC* WASN'T SO HARD TO FIND...

... AN OLD MAN LIVED WITH HIS BEAUTIFUL WIFE ON A FARM.

THEY WERE *HAPPY* TOGETHER, BUT MORE THAN ANYTHING ELSE IN THE WORLD, THEY WANTED A *BABY*.

FOR YEARS AND YEARS, THEY WAITED...

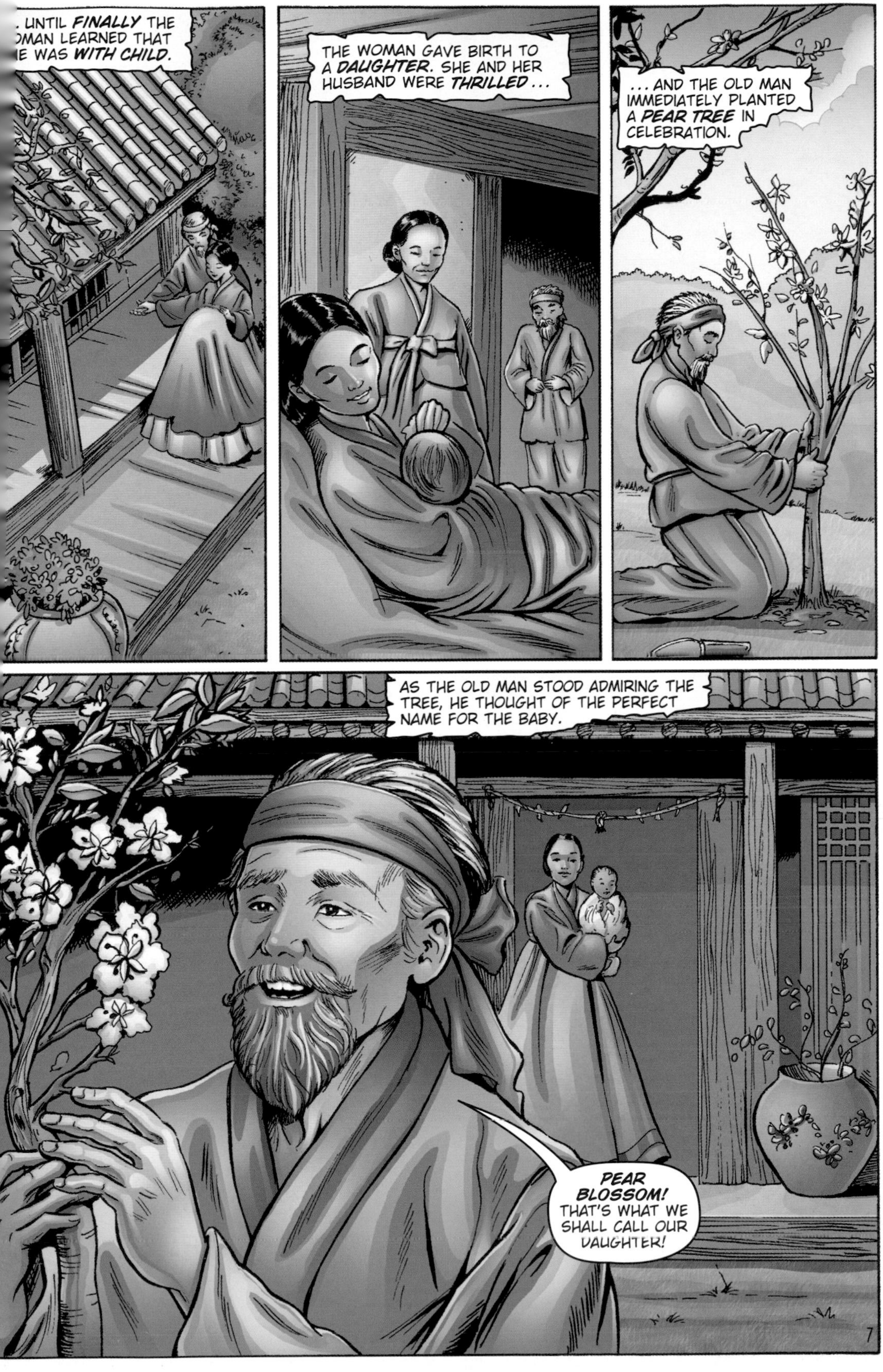
. UNTIL FINALLY THE
OMAN LEARNED THAT
E WAS WITH CHILD.
THE WOMAN GAVE BIRTH TO A DAUGHTER. SHE AND HER HUSBAND WERE THRILLED . . .
. . . AND THE OLD MAN IMMEDIATELY PLANTED A PEAR TREE IN CELEBRATION.
AS THE OLD MAN STOOD ADMIRING THE TREE, HE THOUGHT OF THE PERFECT NAME FOR THE BABY.
PEAR BLOSSOM! THAT'S WHAT WE SHALL CALL OUR DAUGHTER!

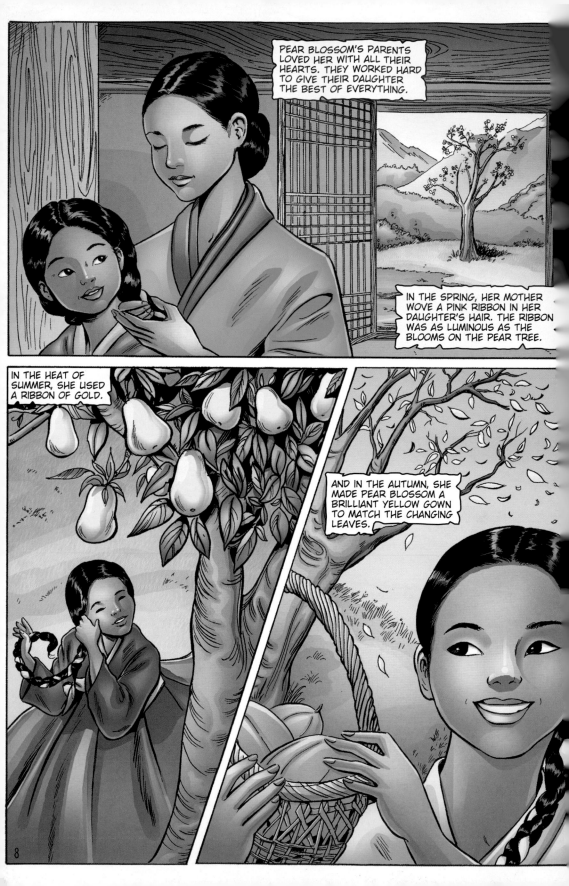

PEAR BLOSSOM'S PARENTS LOVED HER WITH ALL THEIR HEARTS. THEY WORKED HARD TO GIVE THEIR DAUGHTER THE BEST OF EVERYTHING.

IN THE SPRING, HER MOTHER WOVE A PINK RIBBON IN HER DAUGHTER'S HAIR. THE RIBBON WAS AS LUMINOUS AS THE BLOOMS ON THE PEAR TREE.

IN THE HEAT OF SUMMER, SHE USED A RIBBON OF GOLD.

AND IN THE AUTUMN, SHE MADE PEAR BLOSSOM A BRILLIANT YELLOW GOWN TO MATCH THE CHANGING LEAVES.

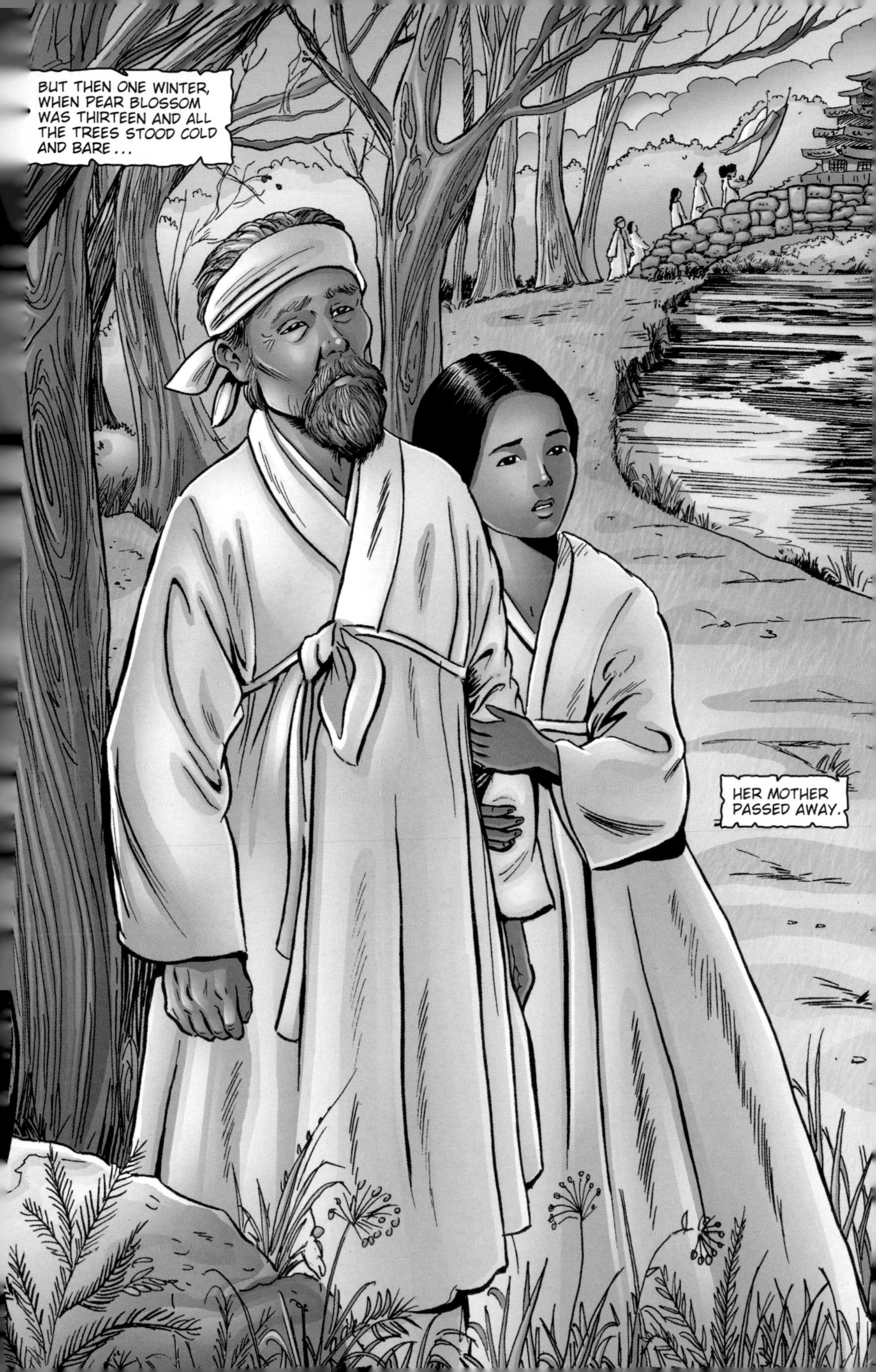
BUT THEN ONE WINTER, WHEN PEAR BLOSSOM WAS THIRTEEN AND ALL THE TREES STOOD COLD AND BARE . . .
HER MOTHER PASSED AWAY.

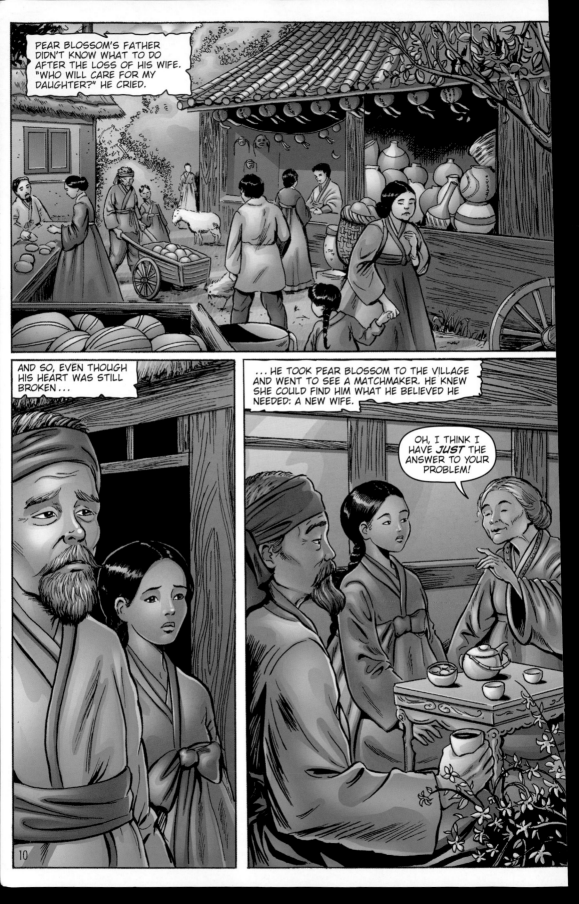

PEAR BLOSSOM'S FATHER DIDN'T KNOW WHAT TO DO AFTER THE LOSS OF HIS WIFE. "WHO WILL CARE FOR MY DAUGHTER?" HE CRIED.

AND SO, EVEN THOUGH HIS HEART WAS STILL BROKEN...

... HE TOOK PEAR BLOSSOM TO THE VILLAGE AND WENT TO SEE A MATCHMAKER. HE KNEW SHE COULD FIND HIM WHAT HE BELIEVED HE NEEDED: A NEW WIFE.

OH, I THINK I HAVE *JUST* THE ANSWER TO YOUR PROBLEM!

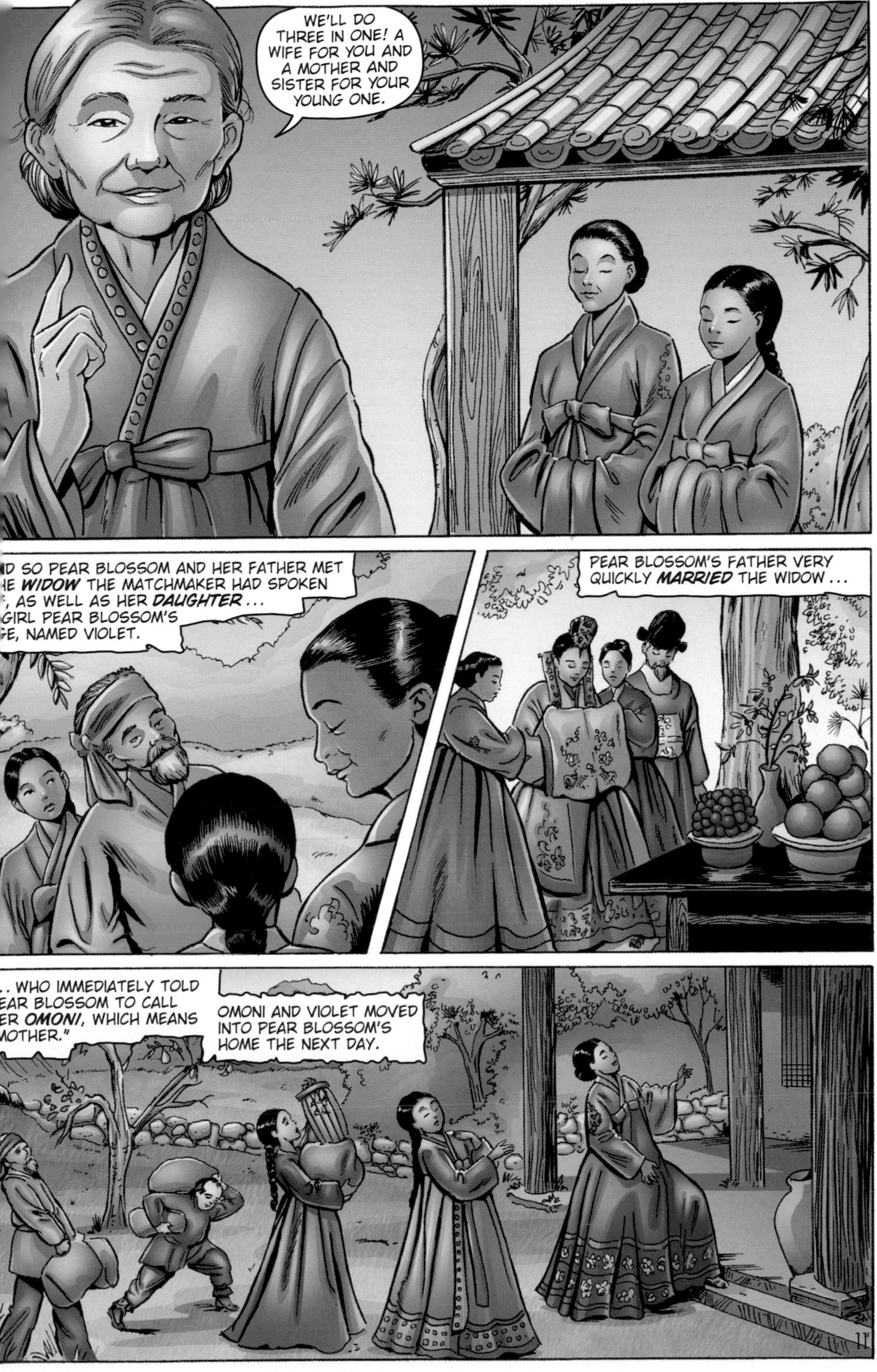

WE'LL DO THREE IN ONE! A WIFE FOR YOU AND A MOTHER AND SISTER FOR YOUR YOUNG ONE.
D SO PEAR BLOSSOM AND HER FATHER MET HE WIDOW THE MATCHMAKER HAD SPOKEN , AS WELL AS HER DAUGHTER ... GIRL PEAR BLOSSOM'S GE, NAMED VIOLET.
PEAR BLOSSOM'S FATHER VERY QUICKLY MARRIED THE WIDOW ...
... WHO IMMEDIATELY TOLD "PEAR BLOSSOM TO CALL HER OMONI, WHICH MEANS MOTHER."
OMONI AND VIOLET MOVED INTO PEAR BLOSSOM'S HOME THE NEXT DAY.

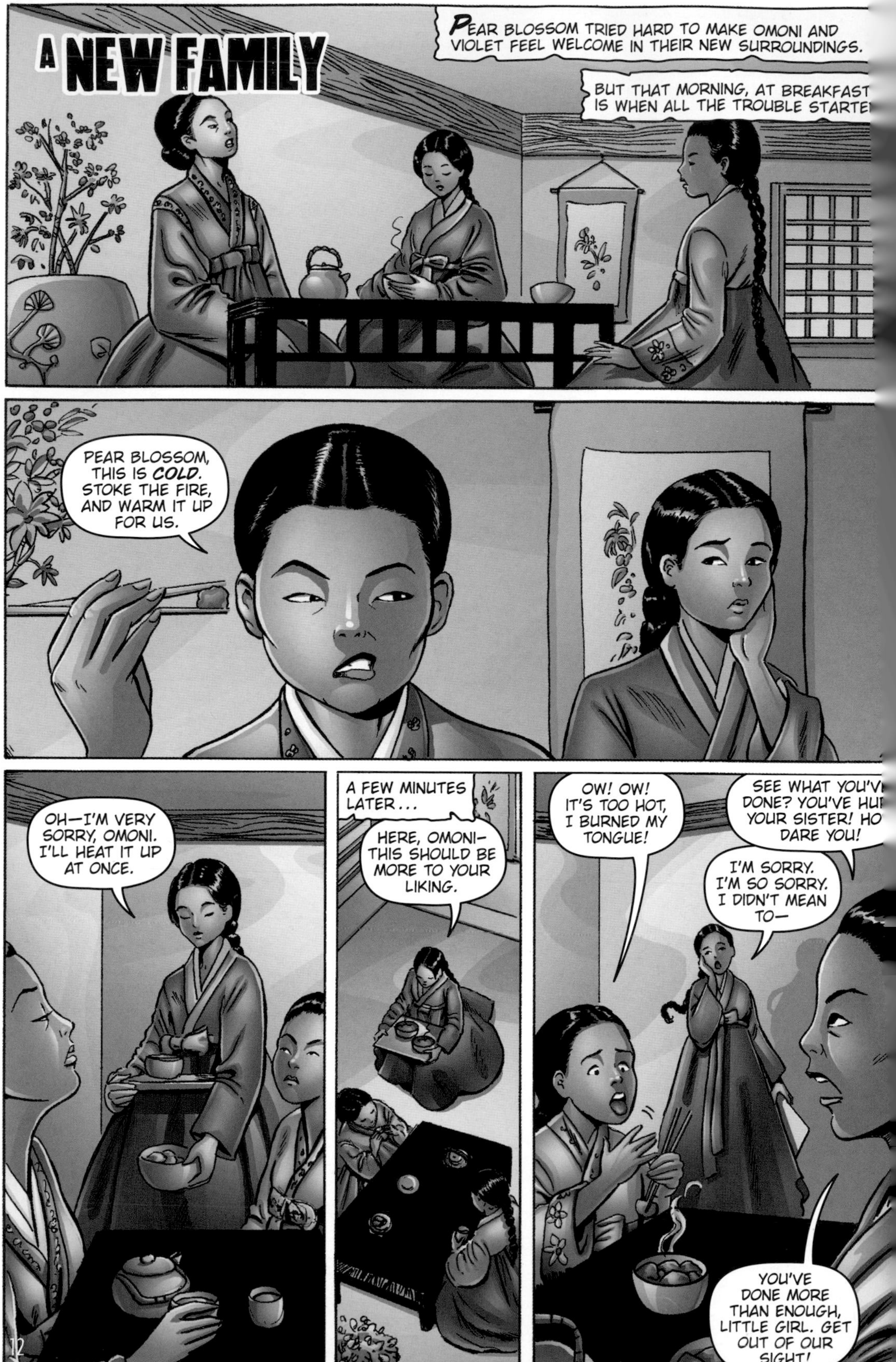
A NEW FAMILY
PEAR BLOSSOM TRIED HARD TO MAKE OMONI AND VIOLET FEEL WELCOME IN THEIR NEW SURROUNDINGS.
BUT THAT MORNING, AT BREAKFAST IS WHEN ALL THE TROUBLE STARTE
PEAR BLOSSOM, THIS IS COLD. STOKE THE FIRE, AND WARM IT UP FOR US.
OH—I'M VERY SORRY, OMONI. I'LL HEAT IT UP AT ONCE.
A FEW MINUTES LATER...
HERE, OMONI– THIS SHOULD BE MORE TO YOUR LIKING.
OW! OW! IT'S TOO HOT, I BURNED MY TONGUE!
SEE WHAT YOU'V DONE? YOU'VE HU YOUR SISTER! HO DARE YOU!
I'M SORRY. I'M SO SORRY. I DIDN'T MEAN TO—
YOU'VE DONE MORE THAN ENOUGH, LITTLE GIRL. GET OUT OF OUR SIGHT!

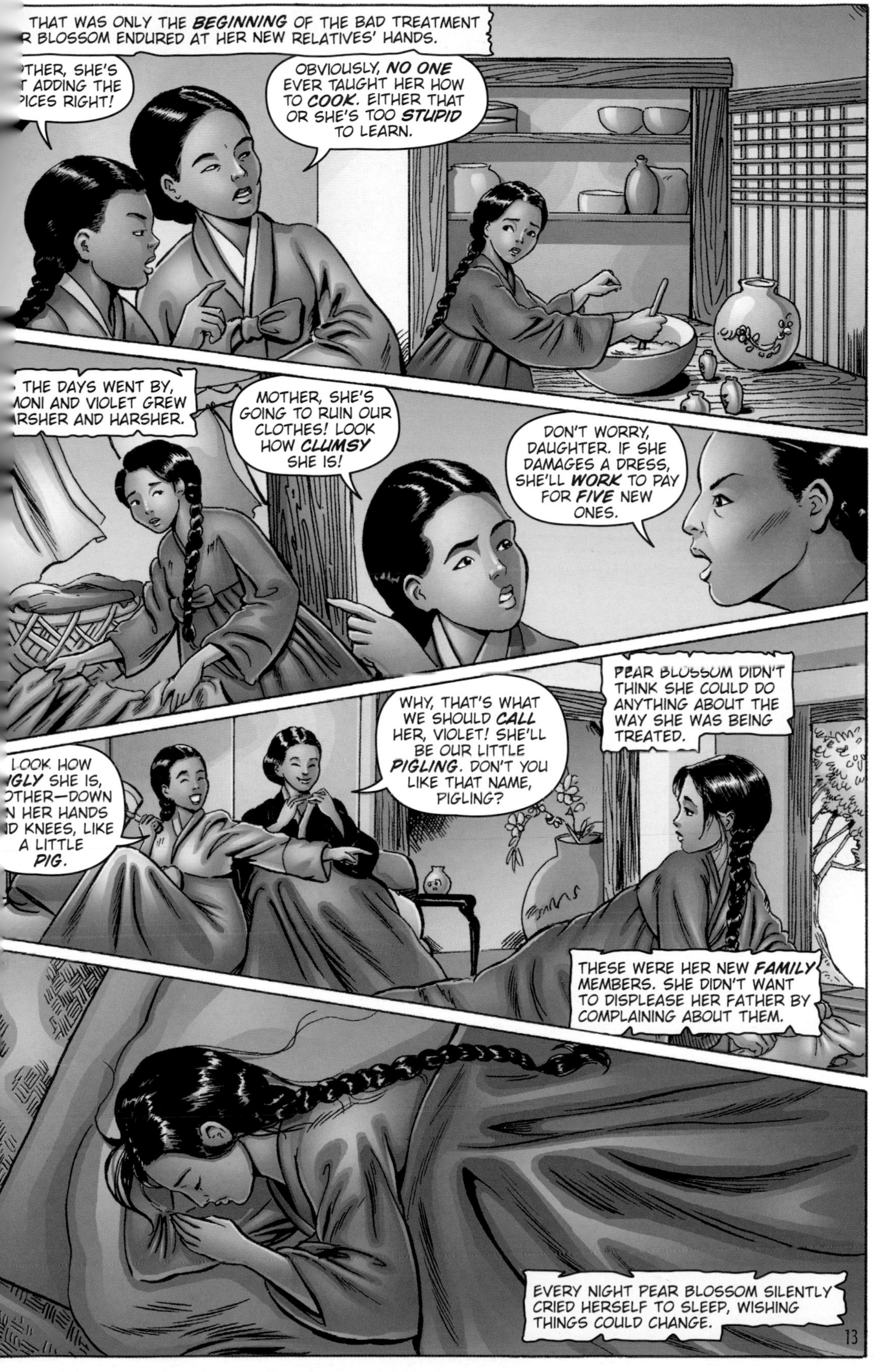
THAT WAS ONLY THE BEGINNING OF THE BAD TREATMENT
R BLOSSOM ENDURED AT HER NEW RELATIVES' HANDS.
OTHER, SHE'S
T ADDING THE
PICES RIGHT!
OBVIOUSLY, NO ONE EVER TAUGHT HER HOW TO COOK. EITHER THAT OR SHE'S TOO STUPID TO LEARN.
THE DAYS WENT BY,
MONI AND VIOLET GREW
ARSHER AND HARSHER.
MOTHER, SHE'S GOING TO RUIN OUR CLOTHES! LOOK HOW CLUMSY SHE IS!
DON'T WORRY, DAUGHTER. IF SHE DAMAGES A DRESS, SHE'LL WORK TO PAY FOR FIVE NEW ONES.
LOOK HOW
IGLY SHE IS,
OTHER—DOWN
N HER HANDS
ND KNEES, LIKE
A LITTLE
PIG.
WHY, THAT'S WHAT WE SHOULD CALL HER, VIOLET! SHE'LL BE OUR LITTLE PIGLING. DON'T YOU LIKE THAT NAME, PIGLING?
PEAR BLOSSOM DIDN'T THINK SHE COULD DO ANYTHING ABOUT THE WAY SHE WAS BEING TREATED.
THESE WERE HER NEW FAMILY MEMBERS. SHE DIDN'T WANT TO DISPLEASE HER FATHER BY COMPLAINING ABOUT THEM.
EVERY NIGHT PEAR BLOSSOM SILENTLY CRIED HERSELF TO SLEEP, WISHING THINGS COULD CHANGE.

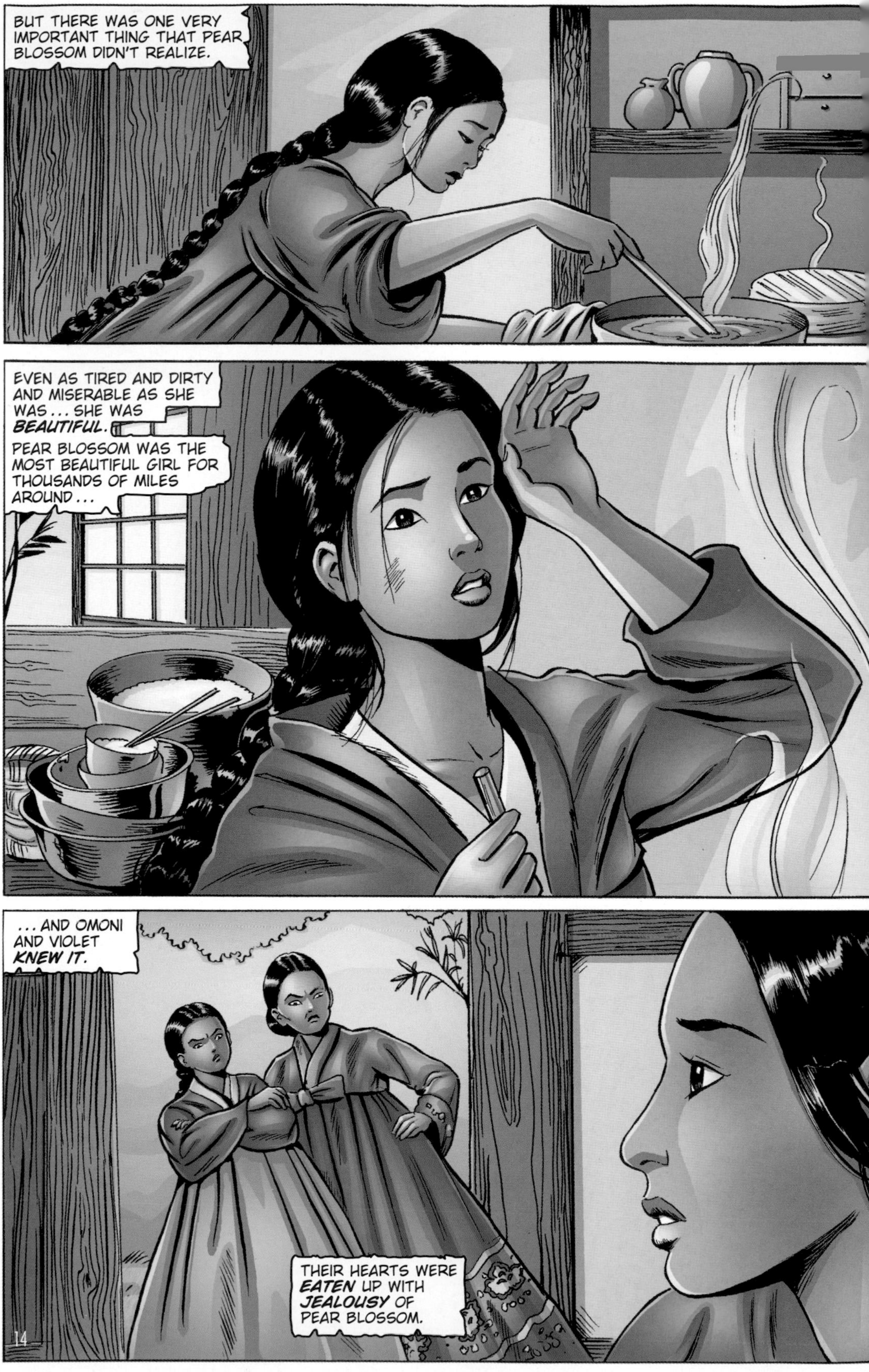
BUT THERE WAS ONE VERY IMPORTANT THING THAT PEAR BLOSSOM DIDN'T REALIZE.
EVEN AS TIRED AND DIRTY AND MISERABLE AS SHE WAS... SHE WAS **BEAUTIFUL**.
PEAR BLOSSOM WAS THE MOST BEAUTIFUL GIRL FOR THOUSANDS OF MILES AROUND...
...AND OMONI AND VIOLET **KNEW IT**.
THEIR HEARTS WERE **EATEN** UP WITH **JEALOUSY** OF PEAR BLOSSOM.

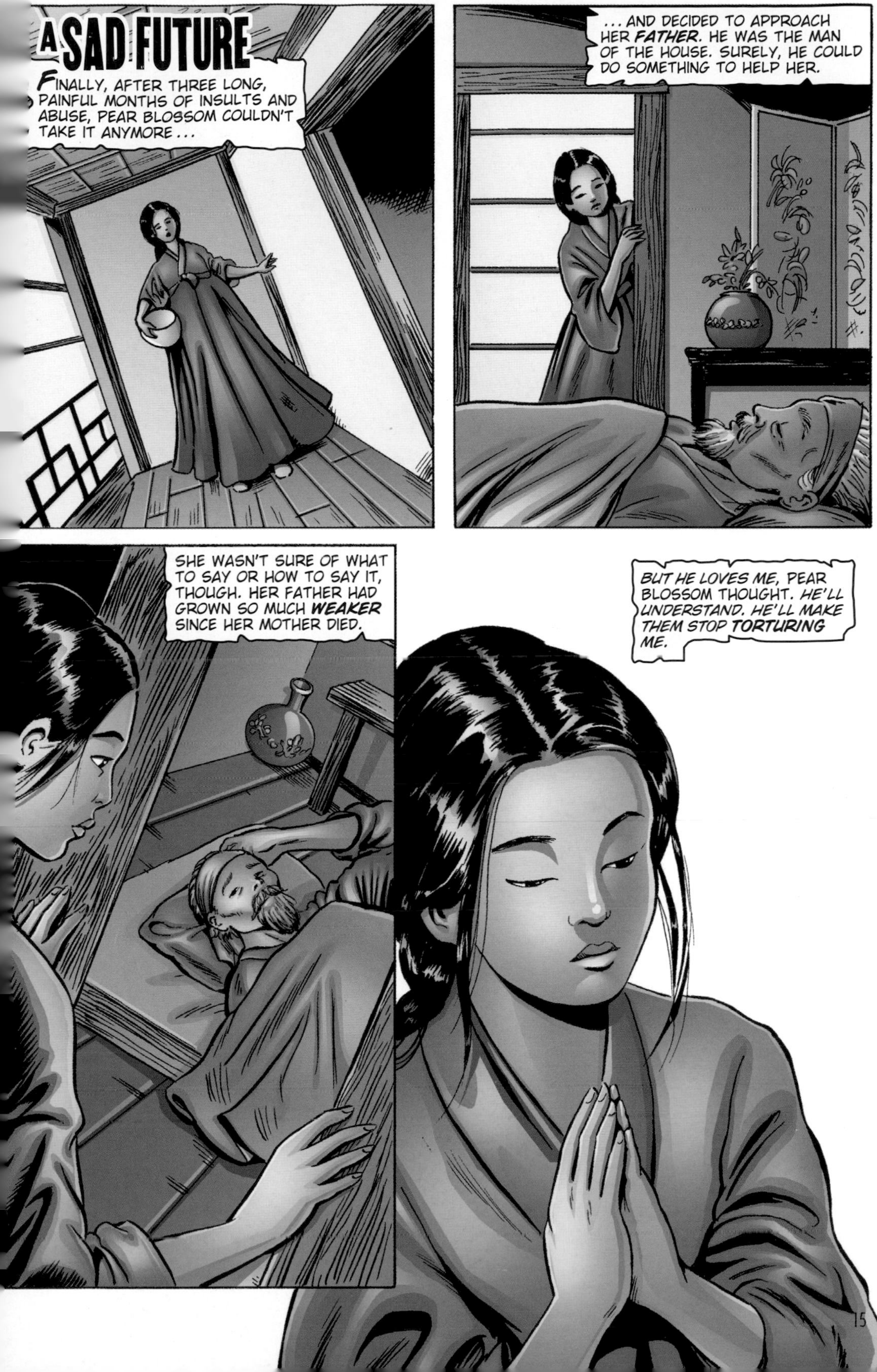
A SAD FUTURE
FINALLY, AFTER THREE LONG, PAINFUL MONTHS OF INSULTS AND ABUSE, PEAR BLOSSOM COULDN'T TAKE IT ANYMORE ...
... AND DECIDED TO APPROACH HER FATHER. HE WAS THE MAN OF THE HOUSE. SURELY, HE COULD DO SOMETHING TO HELP HER.
SHE WASN'T SURE OF WHAT TO SAY OR HOW TO SAY IT, THOUGH. HER FATHER HAD GROWN SO MUCH WEAKER SINCE HER MOTHER DIED.
BUT HE LOVES ME, PEAR BLOSSOM THOUGHT. HE'LL UNDERSTAND. HE'LL MAKE THEM STOP TORTURING ME.

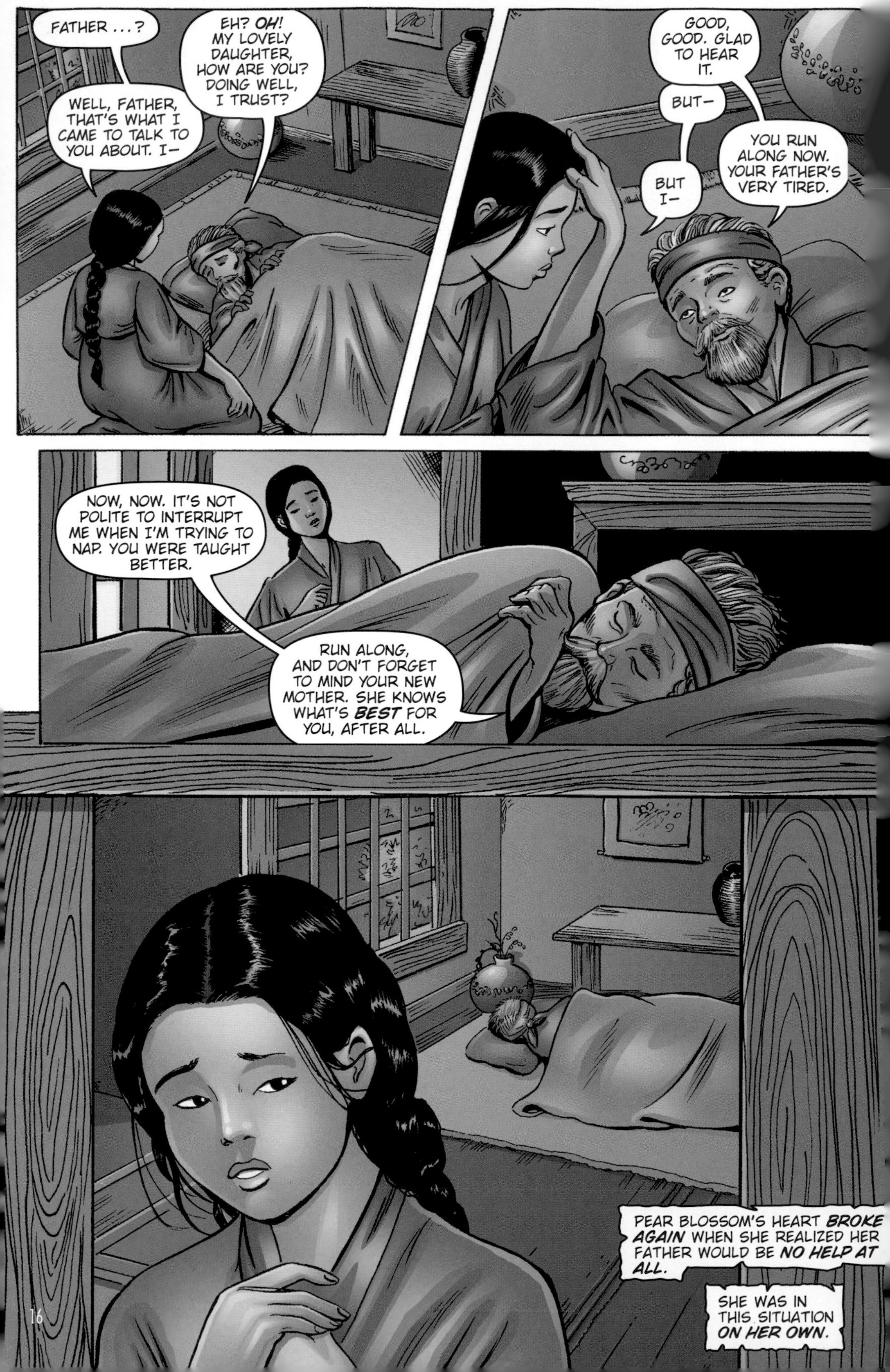
FATHER . . . ?
EH? OH! MY LOVELY DAUGHTER, HOW ARE YOU? DOING WELL, I TRUST?
WELL, FATHER, THAT'S WHAT I CAME TO TALK TO YOU ABOUT. I—
GOOD, GOOD. GLAD TO HEAR IT.
BUT—
YOU RUN ALONG NOW. YOUR FATHER'S VERY TIRED.
BUT I—
NOW, NOW. IT'S NOT POLITE TO INTERRUPT ME WHEN I'M TRYING TO NAP. YOU WERE TAUGHT BETTER.
RUN ALONG, AND DON'T FORGET TO MIND YOUR NEW MOTHER. SHE KNOWS WHAT'S BEST FOR YOU, AFTER ALL.
PEAR BLOSSOM'S HEART BROKE AGAIN WHEN SHE REALIZED HER FATHER WOULD BE NO HELP AT ALL.
SHE WAS IN THIS SITUATION ON HER OWN.

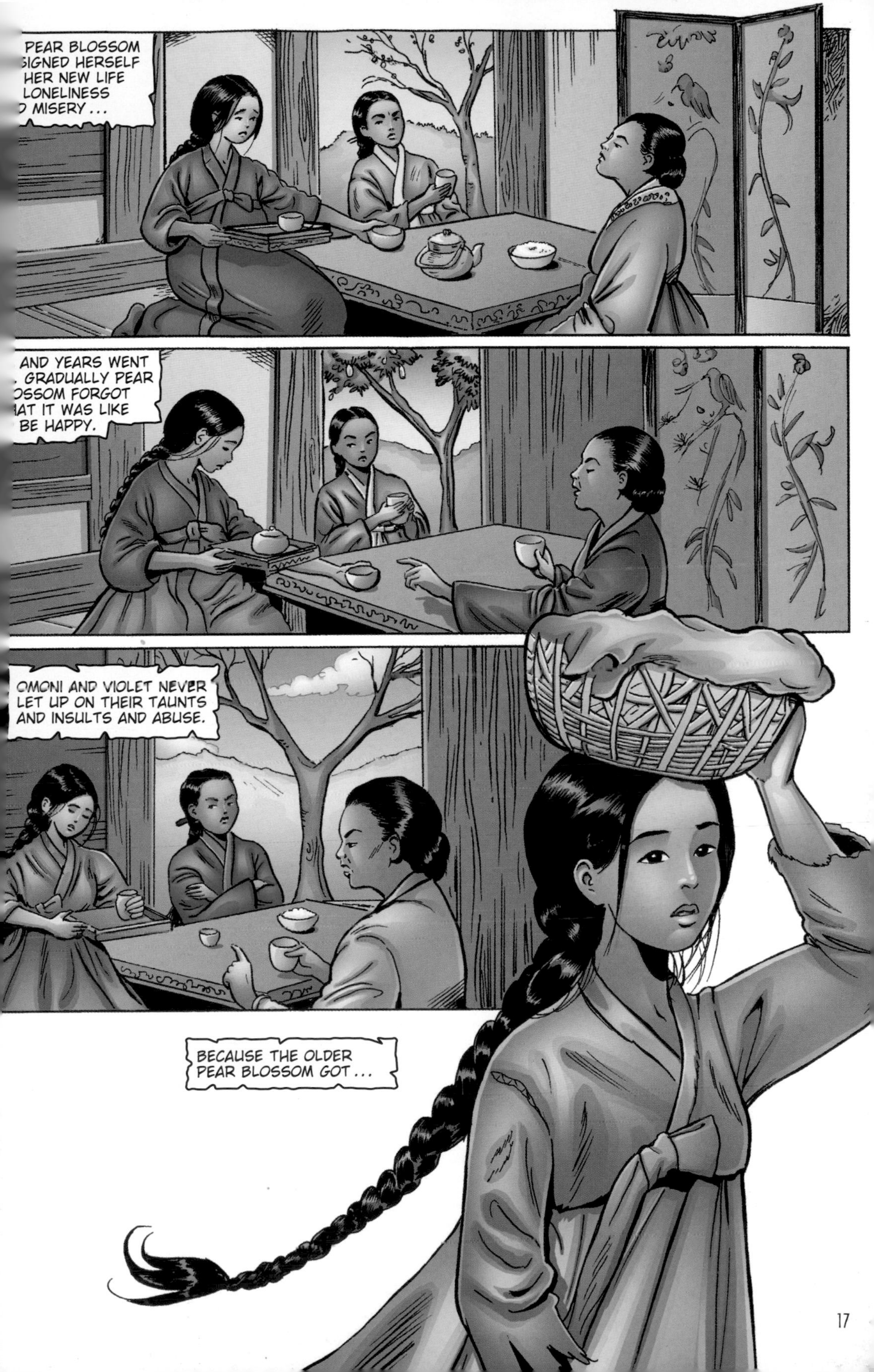
PEAR BLOSSOM
SIGNED HERSELF
HER NEW LIFE
LONELINESS
D MISERY . . .
AND YEARS WENT
. GRADUALLY PEAR
OSSOM FORGOT
AT IT WAS LIKE
BE HAPPY.
OMONI AND VIOLET NEVER LET UP ON THEIR TAUNTS AND INSULTS AND ABUSE.
BECAUSE THE OLDER PEAR BLOSSOM GOT . . .

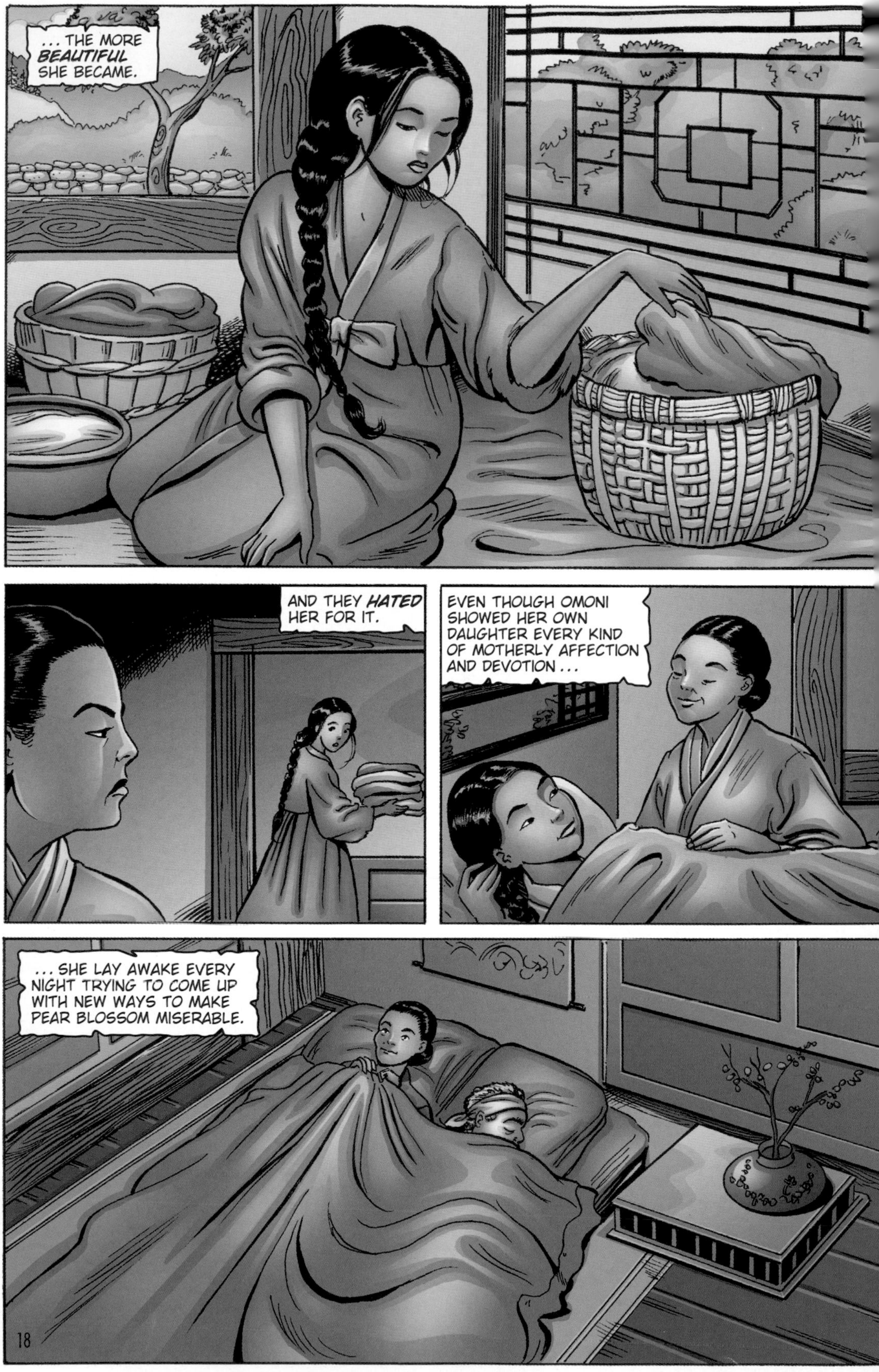

... THE MORE BEAUTIFUL SHE BECAME.
AND THEY HATED HER FOR IT.
EVEN THOUGH OMONI SHOWED HER OWN DAUGHTER EVERY KIND OF MOTHERLY AFFECTION AND DEVOTION ...
... SHE LAY AWAKE EVERY NIGHT TRYING TO COME UP WITH NEW WAYS TO MAKE PEAR BLOSSOM MISERABLE.

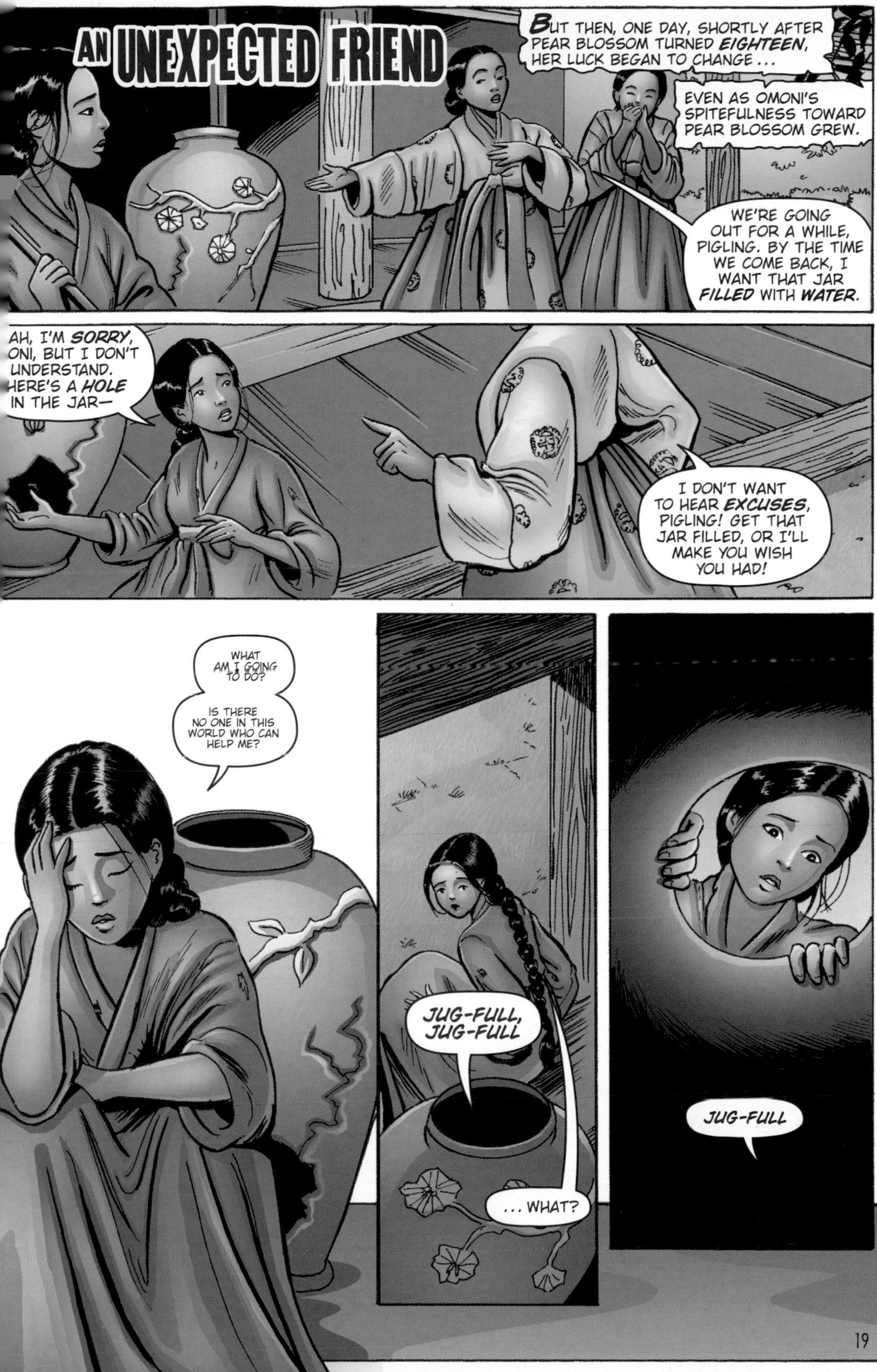
AN UNEXPECTED FRIEND
BUT THEN, ONE DAY, SHORTLY AFTER PEAR BLOSSOM TURNED EIGHTEEN, HER LUCK BEGAN TO CHANGE . . .
EVEN AS OMONI'S SPITEFULNESS TOWARD PEAR BLOSSOM GREW.
WE'RE GOING OUT FOR A WHILE, PIGLING. BY THE TIME WE COME BACK, I WANT THAT JAR FILLED WITH WATER.
AH, I'M SORRY, ONI, BUT I DON'T UNDERSTAND. HERE'S A HOLE IN THE JAR—
I DON'T WANT TO HEAR EXCUSES, PIGLING! GET THAT JAR FILLED, OR I'LL MAKE YOU WISH YOU HAD!
WHAT AM I GOING TO DO?
IS THERE NO ONE IN THIS WORLD WHO CAN HELP ME?
JUG-FULL, JUG-FULL
. . . WHAT?
JUG-FULL

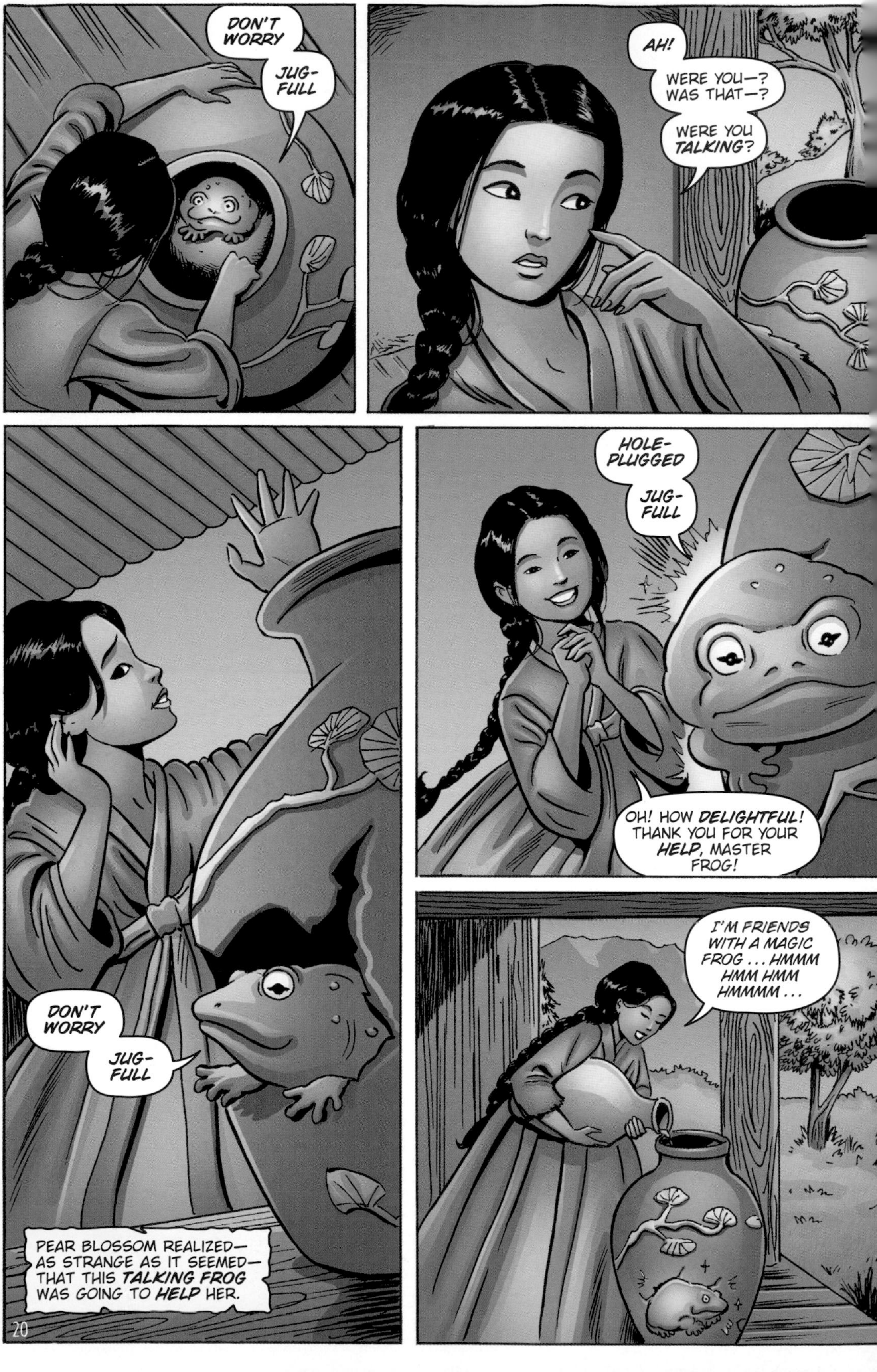
DON'T WORRY
JUG-FULL
AH!
WERE YOU—? WAS THAT—?
WERE YOU TALKING?
HOLE-PLUGGED
JUG-FULL
OH! HOW DELIGHTFUL! THANK YOU FOR YOUR HELP, MASTER FROG!
DON'T WORRY
JUG-FULL
PEAR BLOSSOM REALIZED—AS STRANGE AS IT SEEMED—THAT THIS TALKING FROG WAS GOING TO HELP HER.
I'M FRIENDS WITH A MAGIC FROG . . . HMMM HMM HMM HMMMM . . .

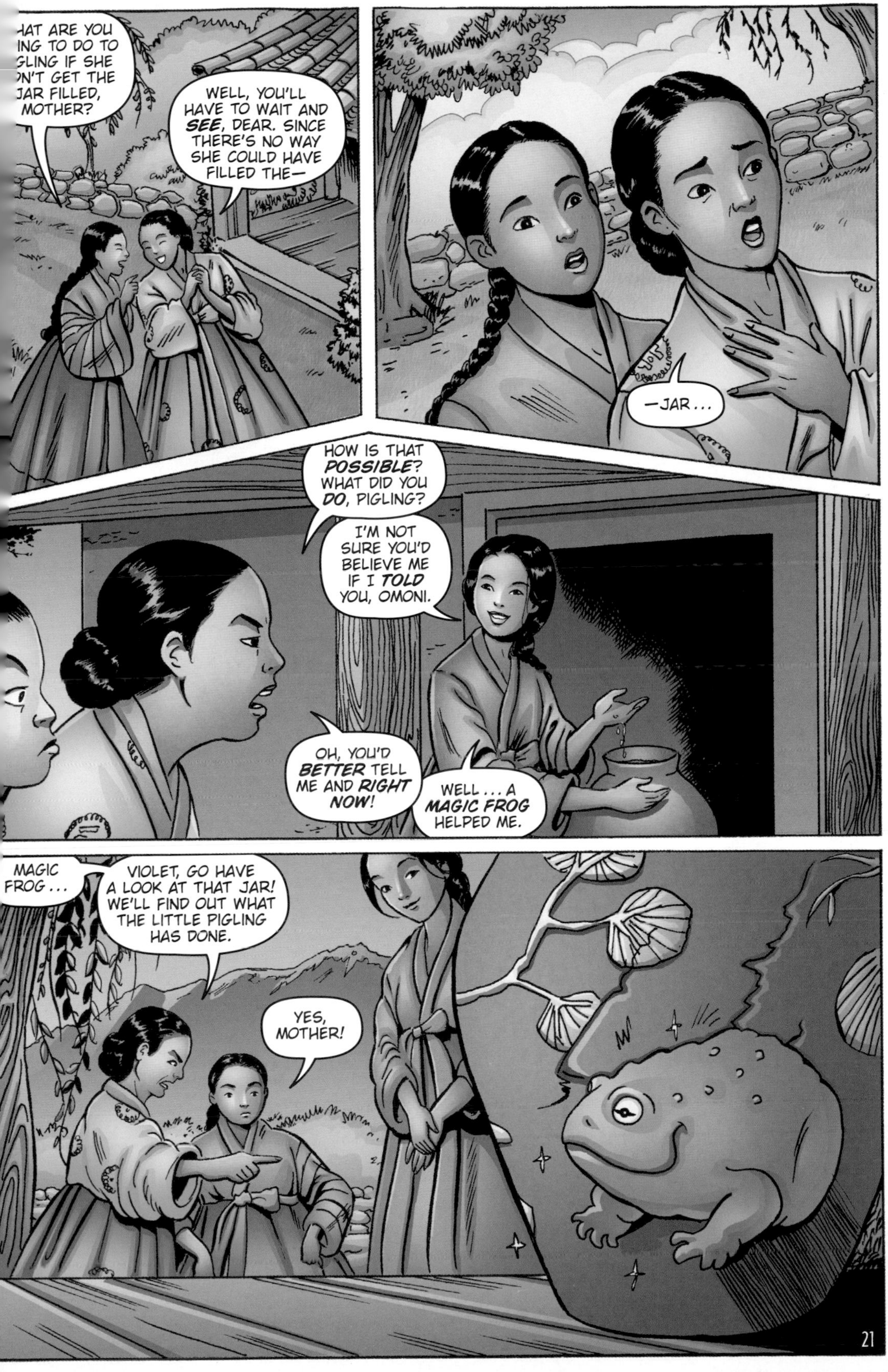
HAT ARE YOU ING TO DO TO GLING IF SHE N'T GET THE JAR FILLED, MOTHER?
WELL, YOU'LL HAVE TO WAIT AND SEE, DEAR. SINCE THERE'S NO WAY SHE COULD HAVE FILLED THE—
—JAR . . .
HOW IS THAT POSSIBLE? WHAT DID YOU DO, PIGLING?
I'M NOT SURE YOU'D BELIEVE ME IF I TOLD YOU, OMONI.
OH, YOU'D BETTER TELL ME AND RIGHT NOW!
WELL . . . A MAGIC FROG HELPED ME.
MAGIC FROG . . .
VIOLET, GO HAVE A LOOK AT THAT JAR! WE'LL FIND OUT WHAT THE LITTLE PIGLING HAS DONE.
YES, MOTHER!

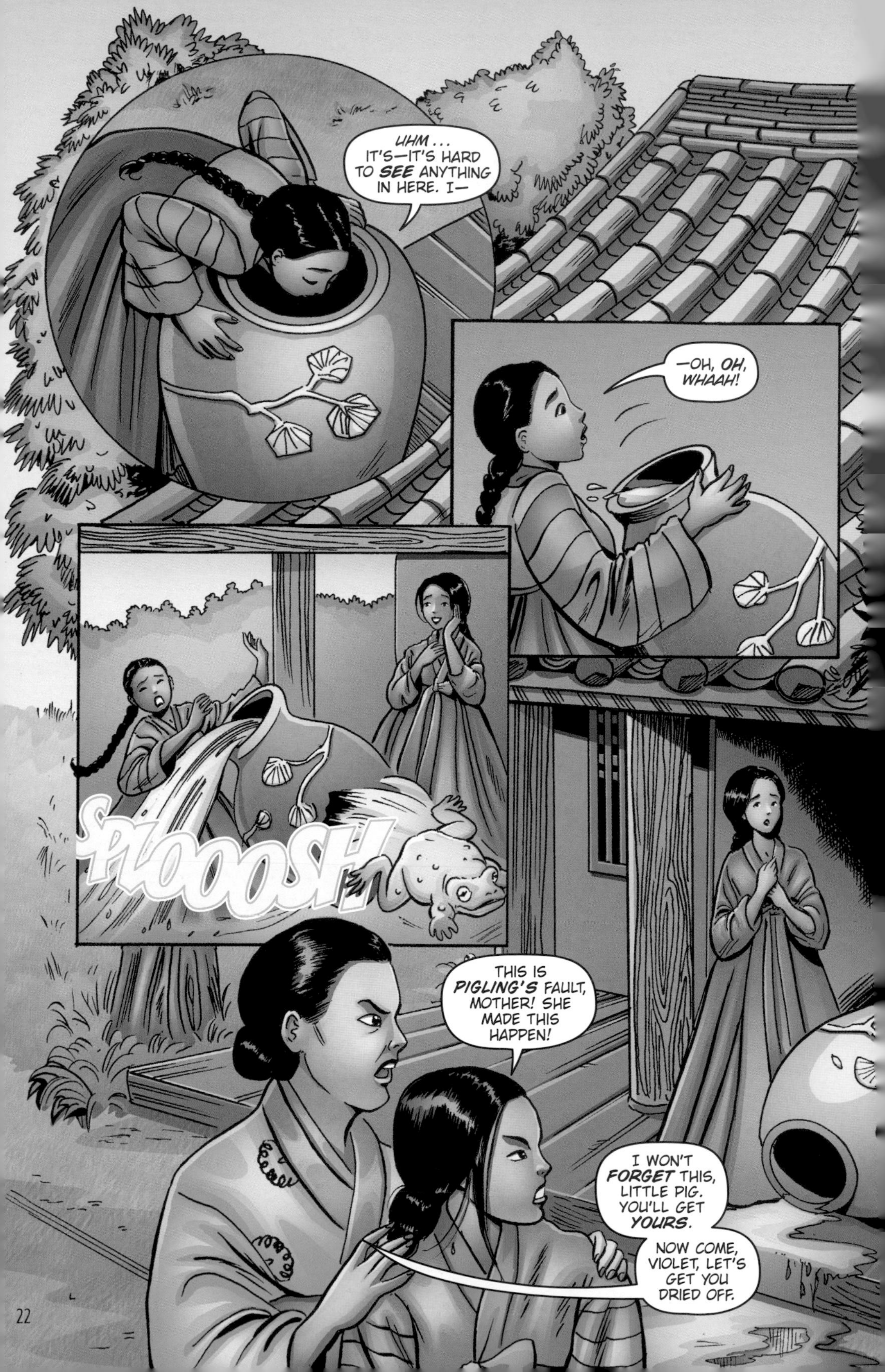
UHM... IT'S—IT'S HARD TO SEE ANYTHING IN HERE. I—
—OH, OH, WHAAH!
SPLOOOSH
THIS IS PIGLING'S FAULT, MOTHER! SHE MADE THIS HAPPEN!
I WON'T FORGET THIS, LITTLE PIG. YOU'LL GET YOURS.
NOW COME, VIOLET, LET'S GET YOU DRIED OFF.

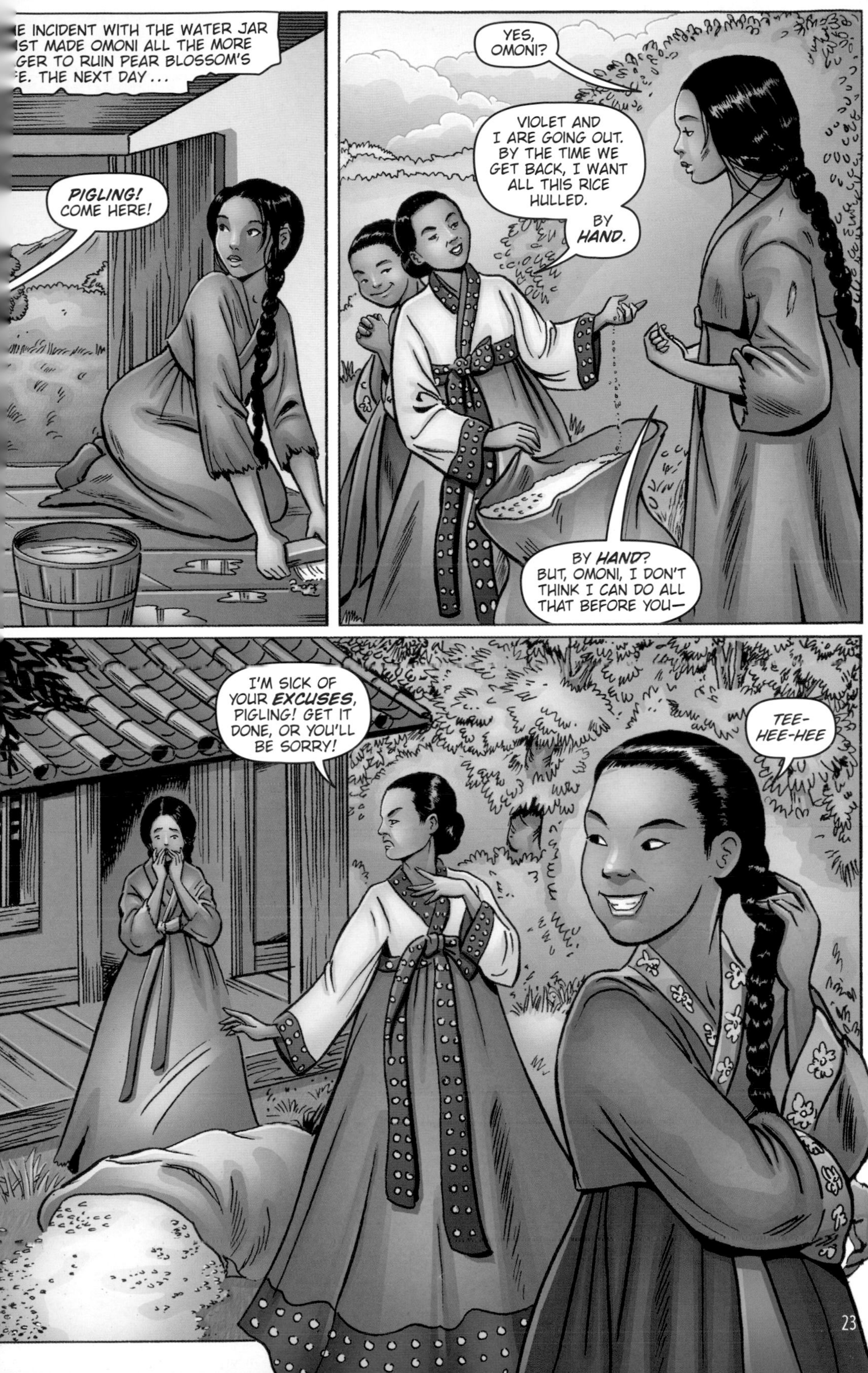
E INCIDENT WITH THE WATER JAR
IST MADE OMONI ALL THE MORE
GER TO RUIN PEAR BLOSSOM'S
FE. THE NEXT DAY . . .
PIGLING! COME HERE!
YES, OMONI?
VIOLET AND I ARE GOING OUT. BY THE TIME WE GET BACK, I WANT ALL THIS RICE HULLED.
BY *HAND*.
BY *HAND*? BUT, OMONI, I DON'T THINK I CAN DO ALL THAT BEFORE YOU—
I'M SICK OF YOUR *EXCUSES*, PIGLING! GET IT DONE, OR YOU'LL BE SORRY!
TEE-HEE-HEE

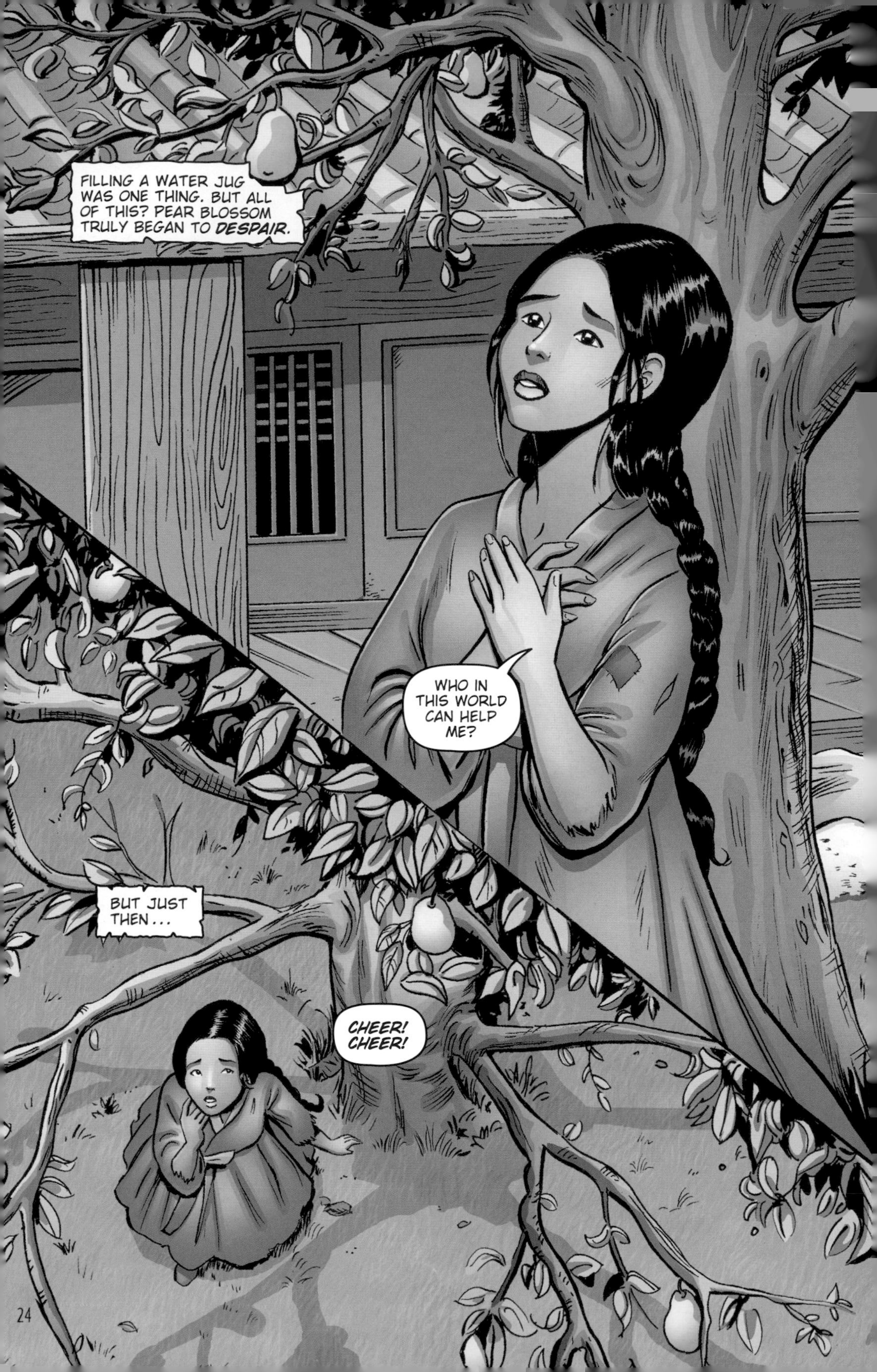
FILLING A WATER JUG WAS ONE THING. BUT ALL OF THIS? PEAR BLOSSOM TRULY BEGAN TO DESPAIR.
WHO IN THIS WORLD CAN HELP ME?
BUT JUST THEN...
CHEER! CHEER!

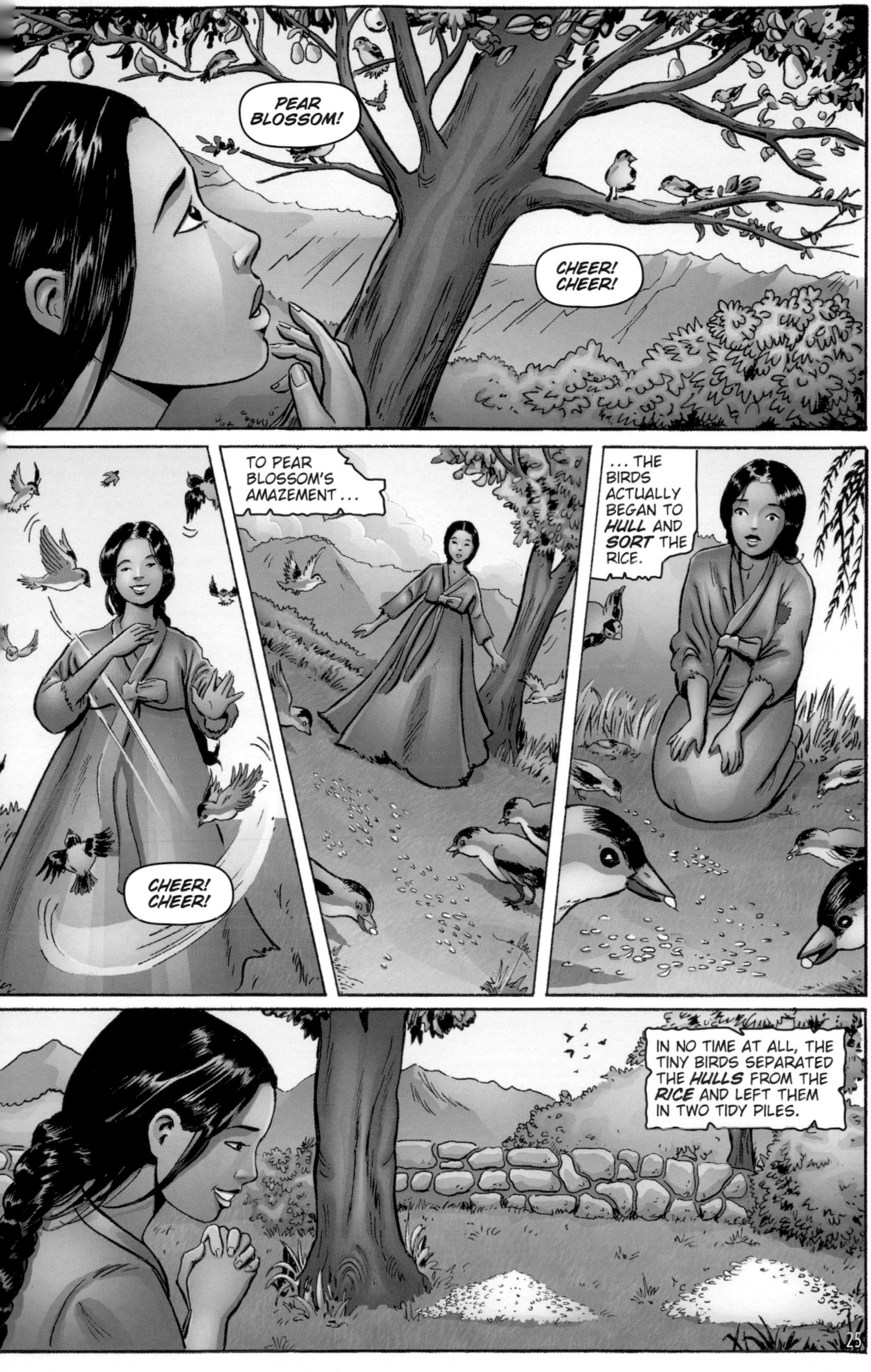
PEAR BLOSSOM!
CHEER! CHEER!
CHEER! CHEER!
TO PEAR BLOSSOM'S AMAZEMENT . . .
. . . THE BIRDS ACTUALLY BEGAN TO HULL AND SORT THE RICE.
IN NO TIME AT ALL, THE TINY BIRDS SEPARATED THE HULLS FROM THE RICE AND LEFT THEM IN TWO TIDY PILES.

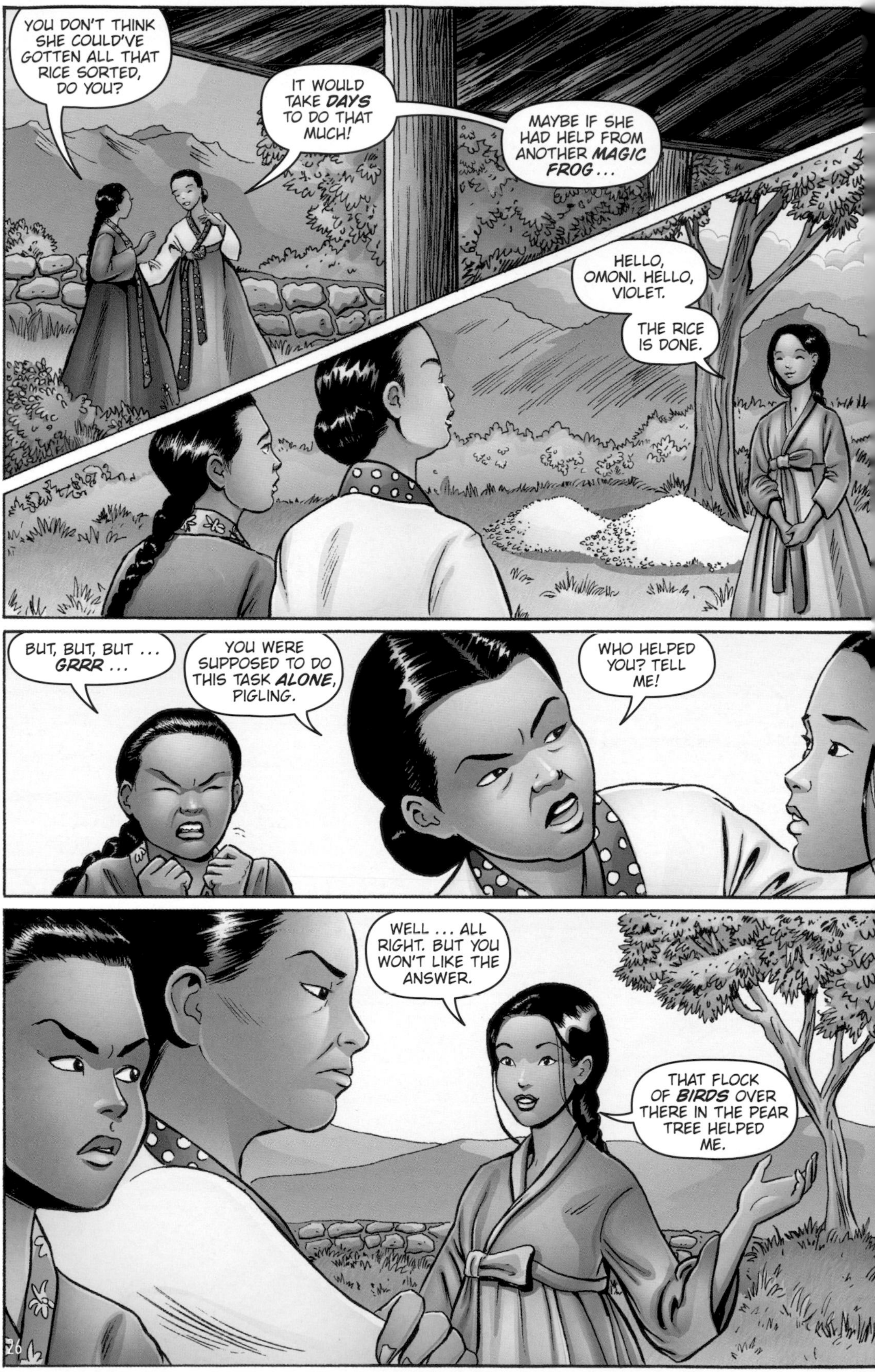
YOU DON'T THINK SHE COULD'VE GOTTEN ALL THAT RICE SORTED, DO YOU?
IT WOULD TAKE DAYS TO DO THAT MUCH!
MAYBE IF SHE HAD HELP FROM ANOTHER MAGIC FROG . . .
HELLO, OMONI. HELLO, VIOLET.
THE RICE IS DONE.
BUT, BUT, BUT . . . GRRR . . .
YOU WERE SUPPOSED TO DO THIS TASK ALONE, PIGLING.
WHO HELPED YOU? TELL ME!
WELL . . . ALL RIGHT. BUT YOU WON'T LIKE THE ANSWER.
THAT FLOCK OF BIRDS OVER THERE IN THE PEAR TREE HELPED ME.

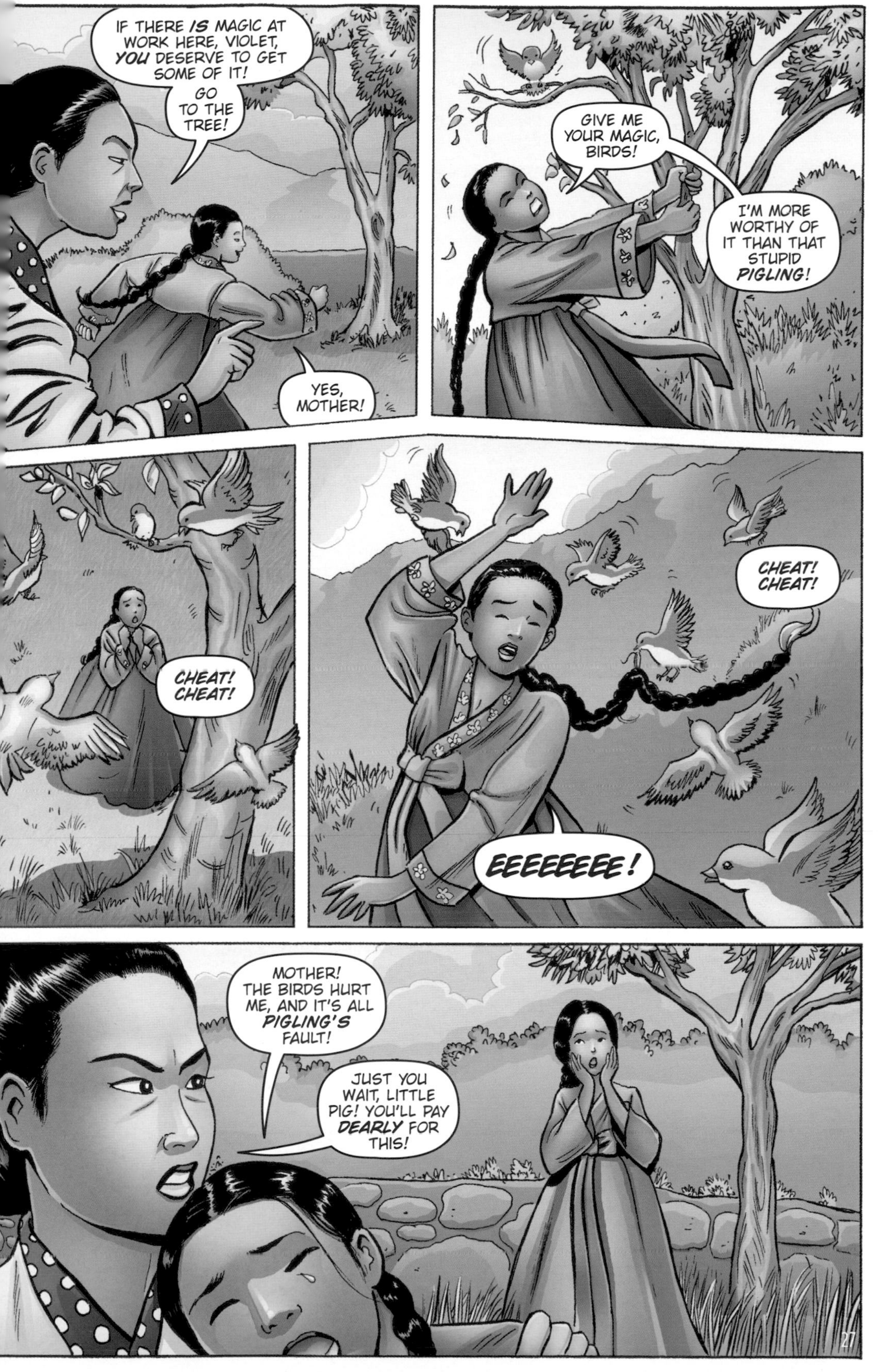
IF THERE *IS* MAGIC AT WORK HERE, VIOLET, ***YOU*** DESERVE TO GET SOME OF IT!
GO TO THE TREE!
YES, MOTHER!
GIVE ME YOUR MAGIC, BIRDS!
I'M MORE WORTHY OF IT THAN THAT STUPID ***PIGLING***!
CHEAT! CHEAT!
CHEAT! CHEAT!
EEEEEEEE!
MOTHER! THE BIRDS HURT ME, AND IT'S ALL ***PIGLING'S*** FAULT!
JUST YOU WAIT, LITTLE PIG! YOU'LL PAY ***DEARLY*** FOR THIS!

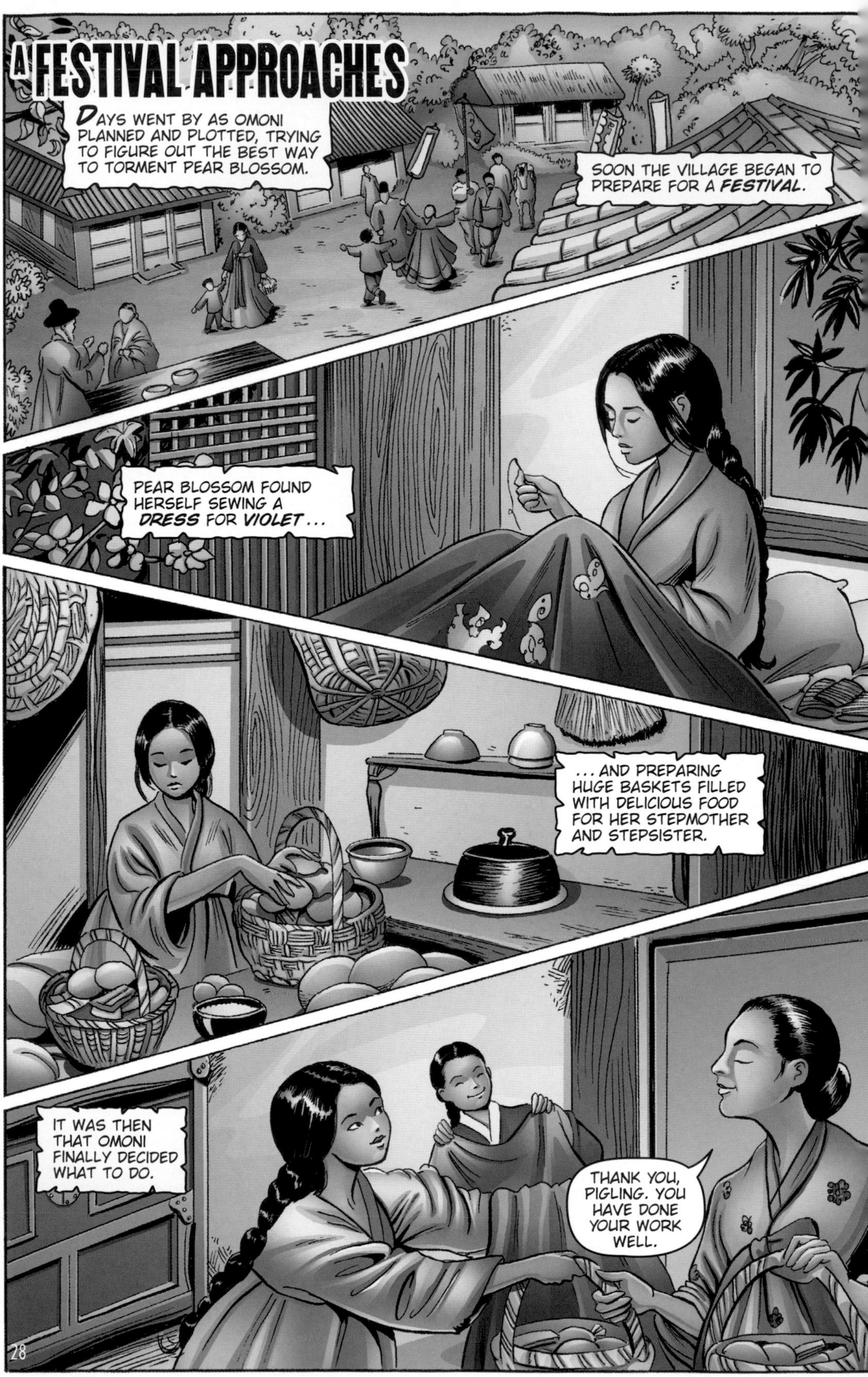

A FESTIVAL APPROACHES
DAYS WENT BY AS OMONI PLANNED AND PLOTTED, TRYING TO FIGURE OUT THE BEST WAY TO TORMENT PEAR BLOSSOM.
SOON THE VILLAGE BEGAN TO PREPARE FOR A FESTIVAL.
PEAR BLOSSOM FOUND HERSELF SEWING A DRESS FOR VIOLET . . .
. . . AND PREPARING HUGE BASKETS FILLED WITH DELICIOUS FOOD FOR HER STEPMOTHER AND STEPSISTER.
IT WAS THEN THAT OMONI FINALLY DECIDED WHAT TO DO.
THANK YOU, PIGLING. YOU HAVE DONE YOUR WORK WELL.

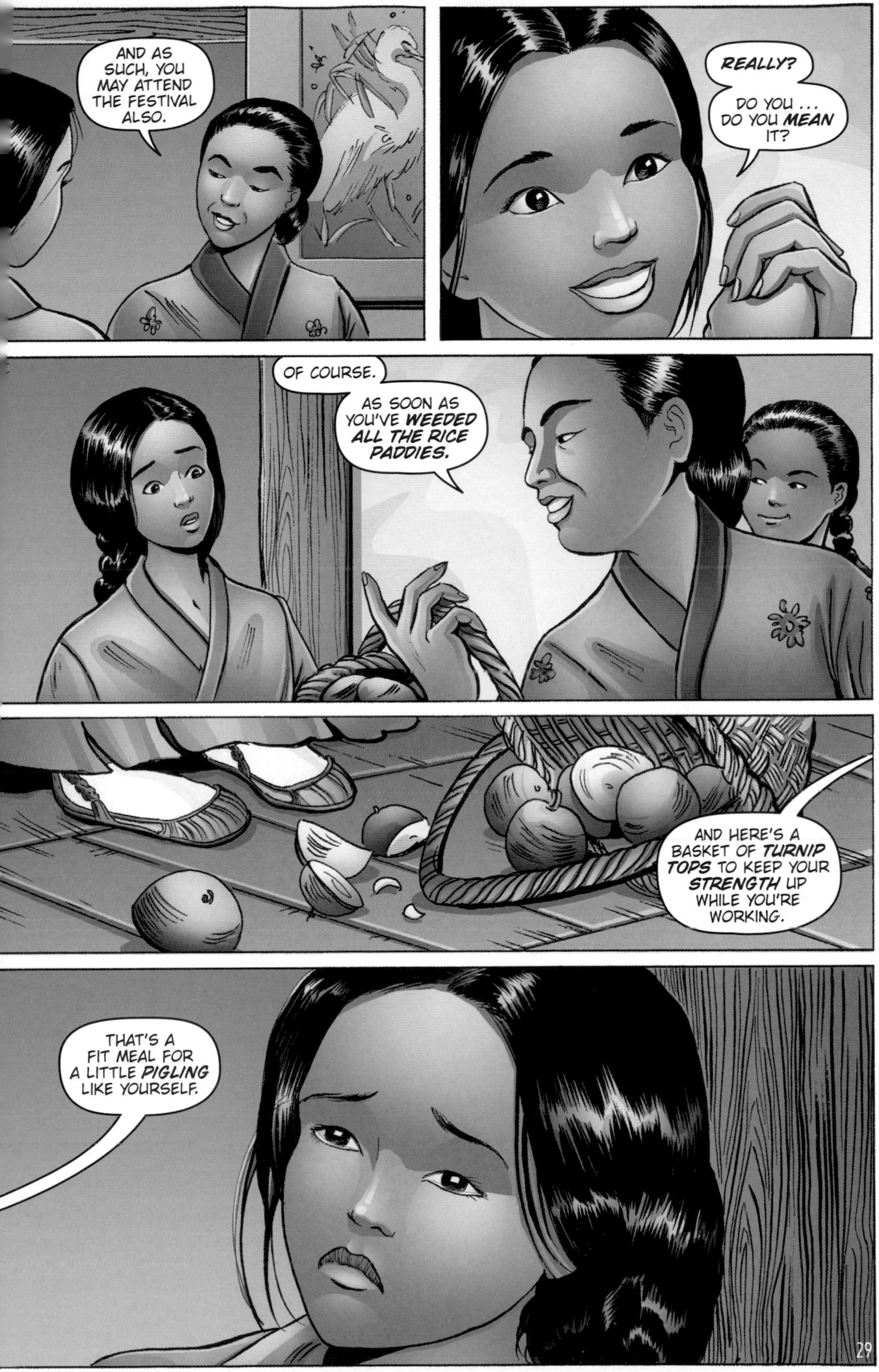
AND AS SUCH, YOU MAY ATTEND THE FESTIVAL ALSO.
REALLY?
DO YOU . . . DO YOU MEAN IT?
OF COURSE.
AS SOON AS YOU'VE WEEDED ALL THE RICE PADDIES.
AND HERE'S A BASKET OF TURNIP TOPS TO KEEP YOUR STRENGTH UP WHILE YOU'RE WORKING.
THAT'S A FIT MEAL FOR A LITTLE PIGLING LIKE YOURSELF.

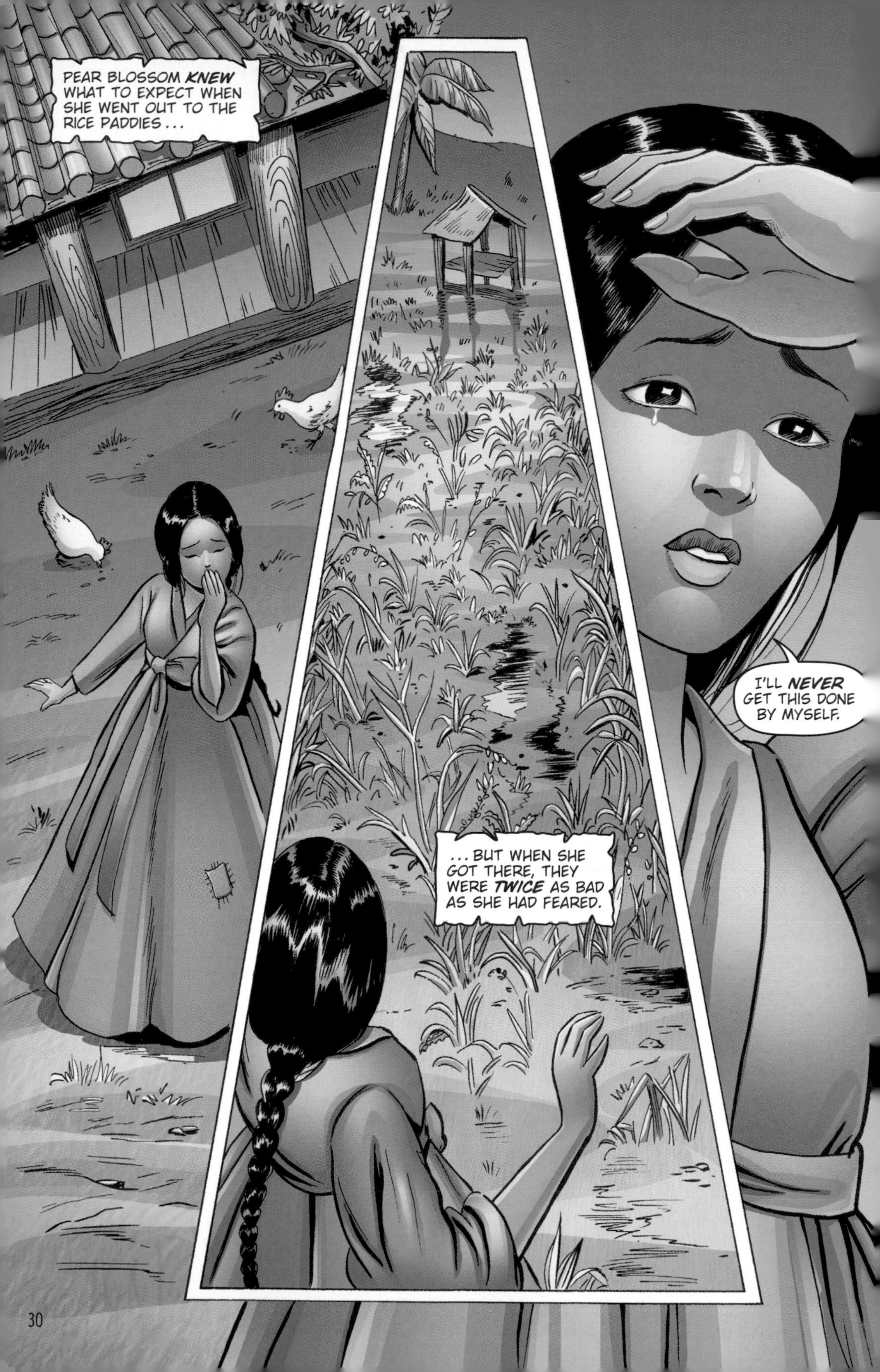
PEAR BLOSSOM KNEW WHAT TO EXPECT WHEN SHE WENT OUT TO THE RICE PADDIES . . .
. . . BUT WHEN SHE GOT THERE, THEY WERE TWICE AS BAD AS SHE HAD FEARED.
I'LL NEVER GET THIS DONE BY MYSELF.

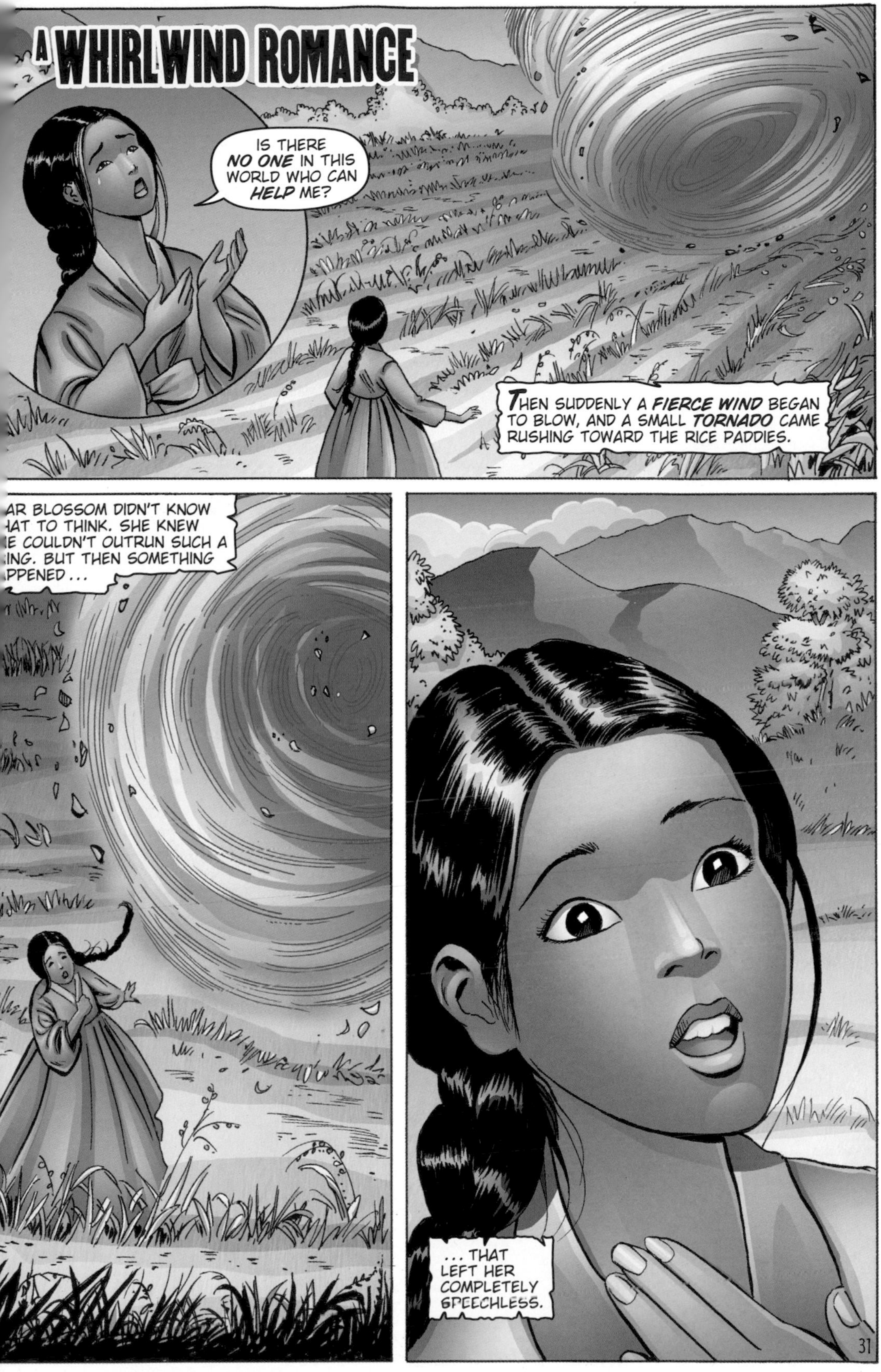

A WHIRLWIND ROMANCE
IS THERE NO ONE IN THIS WORLD WHO CAN HELP ME?
THEN SUDDENLY A FIERCE WIND BEGAN TO BLOW, AND A SMALL TORNADO CAME RUSHING TOWARD THE RICE PADDIES.
AR BLOSSOM DIDN'T KNOW
HAT TO THINK. SHE KNEW
E COULDN'T OUTRUN SUCH A
ING. BUT THEN SOMETHING
PPENED . . .
. . . THAT LEFT HER COMPLETELY SPEECHLESS.

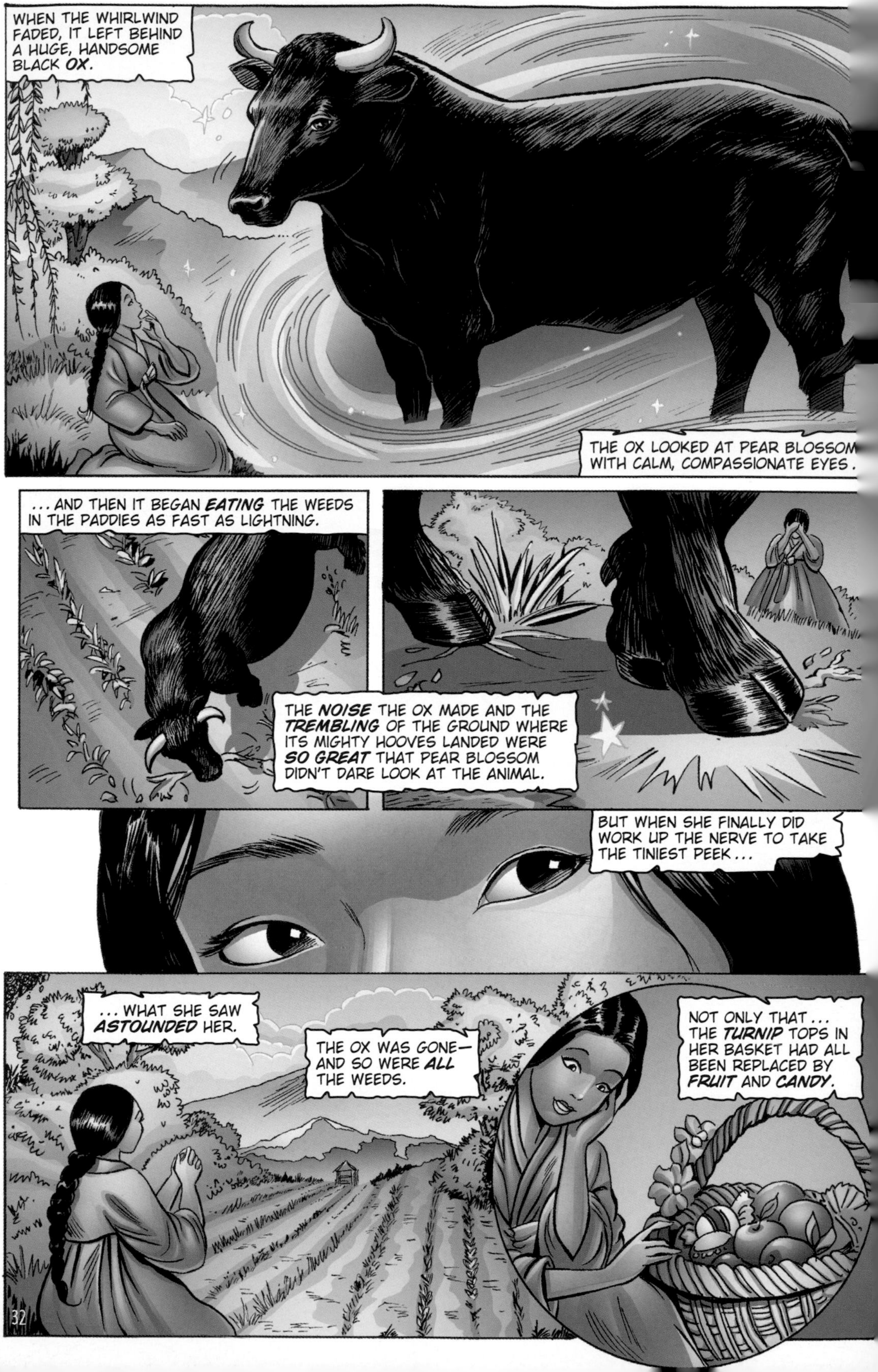
WHEN THE WHIRLWIND FADED, IT LEFT BEHIND A HUGE, HANDSOME BLACK OX.
THE OX LOOKED AT PEAR BLOSSOM WITH CALM, COMPASSIONATE EYES . .
. . . AND THEN IT BEGAN EATING THE WEEDS IN THE PADDIES AS FAST AS LIGHTNING.
THE NOISE THE OX MADE AND THE TREMBLING OF THE GROUND WHERE ITS MIGHTY HOOVES LANDED WERE SO GREAT THAT PEAR BLOSSOM DIDN'T DARE LOOK AT THE ANIMAL.
BUT WHEN SHE FINALLY DID WORK UP THE NERVE TO TAKE THE TINIEST PEEK . . .
. . . WHAT SHE SAW ASTOUNDED HER.
THE OX WAS GONE— AND SO WERE ALL THE WEEDS.
NOT ONLY THAT . . . THE TURNIP TOPS IN HER BASKET HAD ALL BEEN REPLACED BY FRUIT AND CANDY.

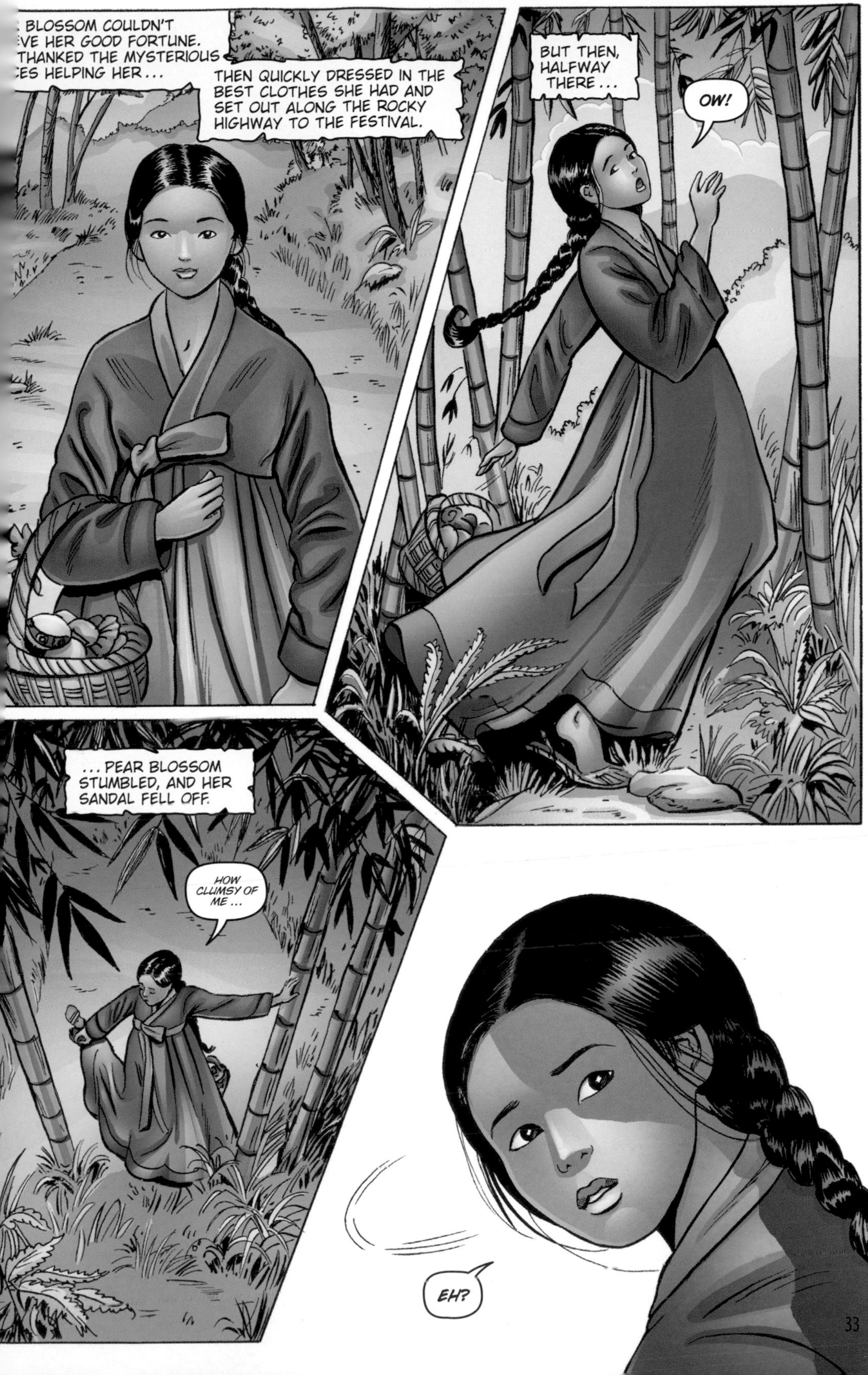

BLOSSOM COULDN'T
EVE HER GOOD FORTUNE.
THANKED THE MYSTERIOUS
CES HELPING HER...
THEN QUICKLY DRESSED IN THE BEST CLOTHES SHE HAD AND SET OUT ALONG THE ROCKY HIGHWAY TO THE FESTIVAL.
BUT THEN, HALFWAY THERE...
OW!
...PEAR BLOSSOM STUMBLED, AND HER SANDAL FELL OFF.
HOW CLUMSY OF ME...
EH?

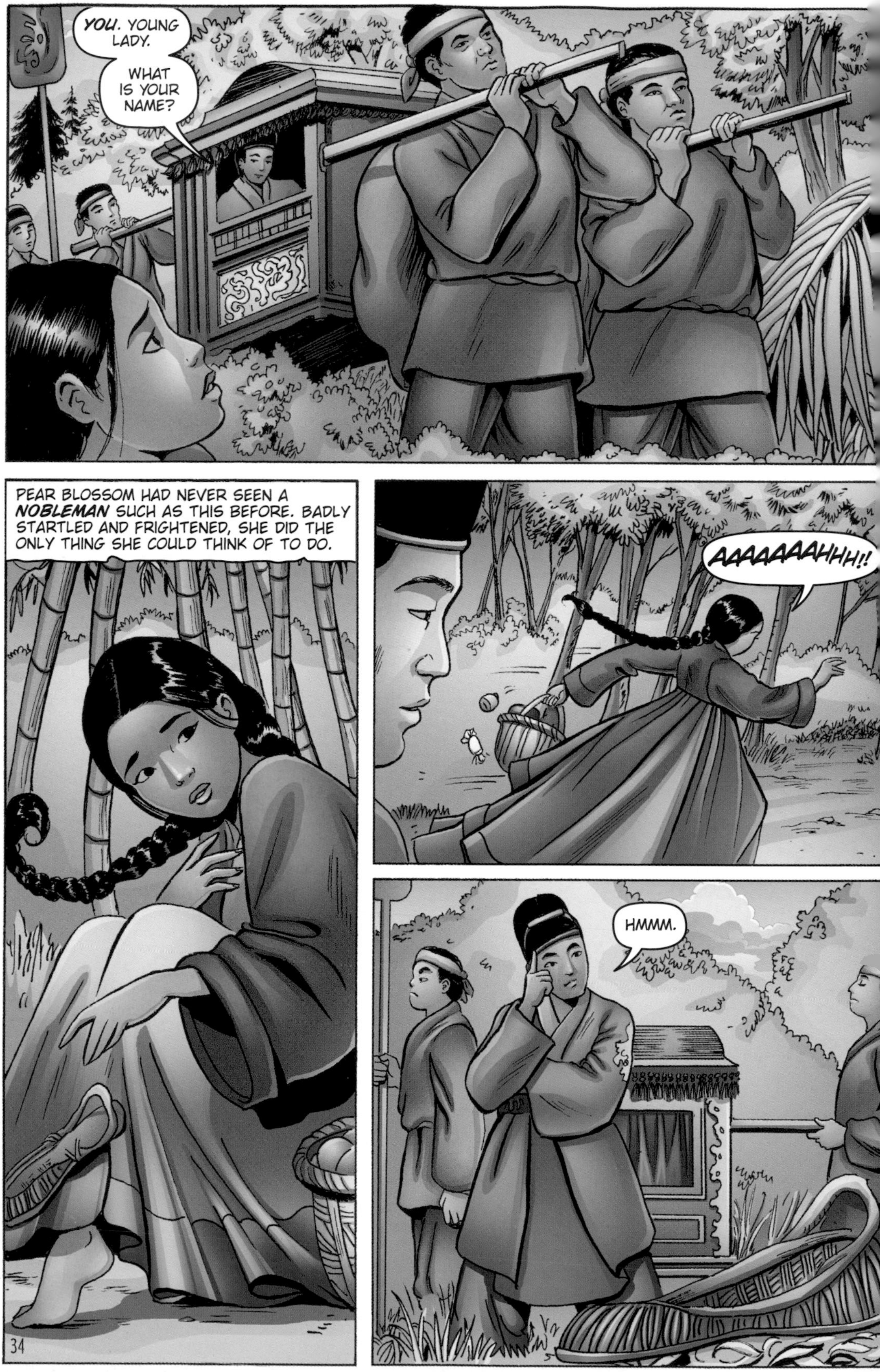

YOU. YOUNG LADY.
WHAT IS YOUR NAME?
PEAR BLOSSOM HAD NEVER SEEN A NOBLEMAN SUCH AS THIS BEFORE. BADLY STARTLED AND FRIGHTENED, SHE DID THE ONLY THING SHE COULD THINK OF TO DO.
AAAAAAAHHH!!
HMMM.

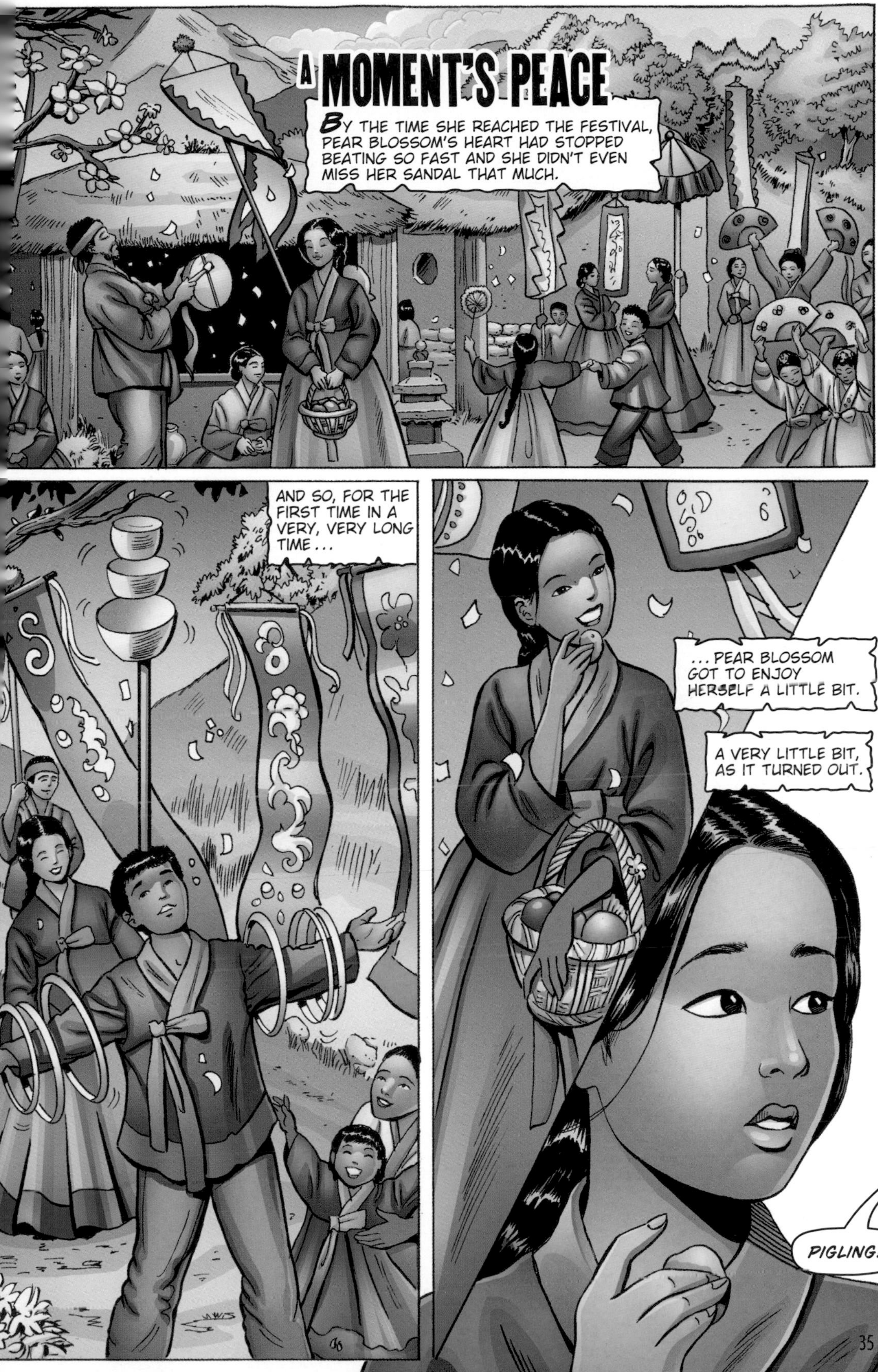
A MOMENT'S PEACE
BY THE TIME SHE REACHED THE FESTIVAL, PEAR BLOSSOM'S HEART HAD STOPPED BEATING SO FAST AND SHE DIDN'T EVEN MISS HER SANDAL THAT MUCH.
AND SO, FOR THE FIRST TIME IN A VERY, VERY LONG TIME . . .
. . . PEAR BLOSSOM GOT TO ENJOY HERSELF A LITTLE BIT.
A VERY LITTLE BIT, AS IT TURNED OUT.
PIGLING!

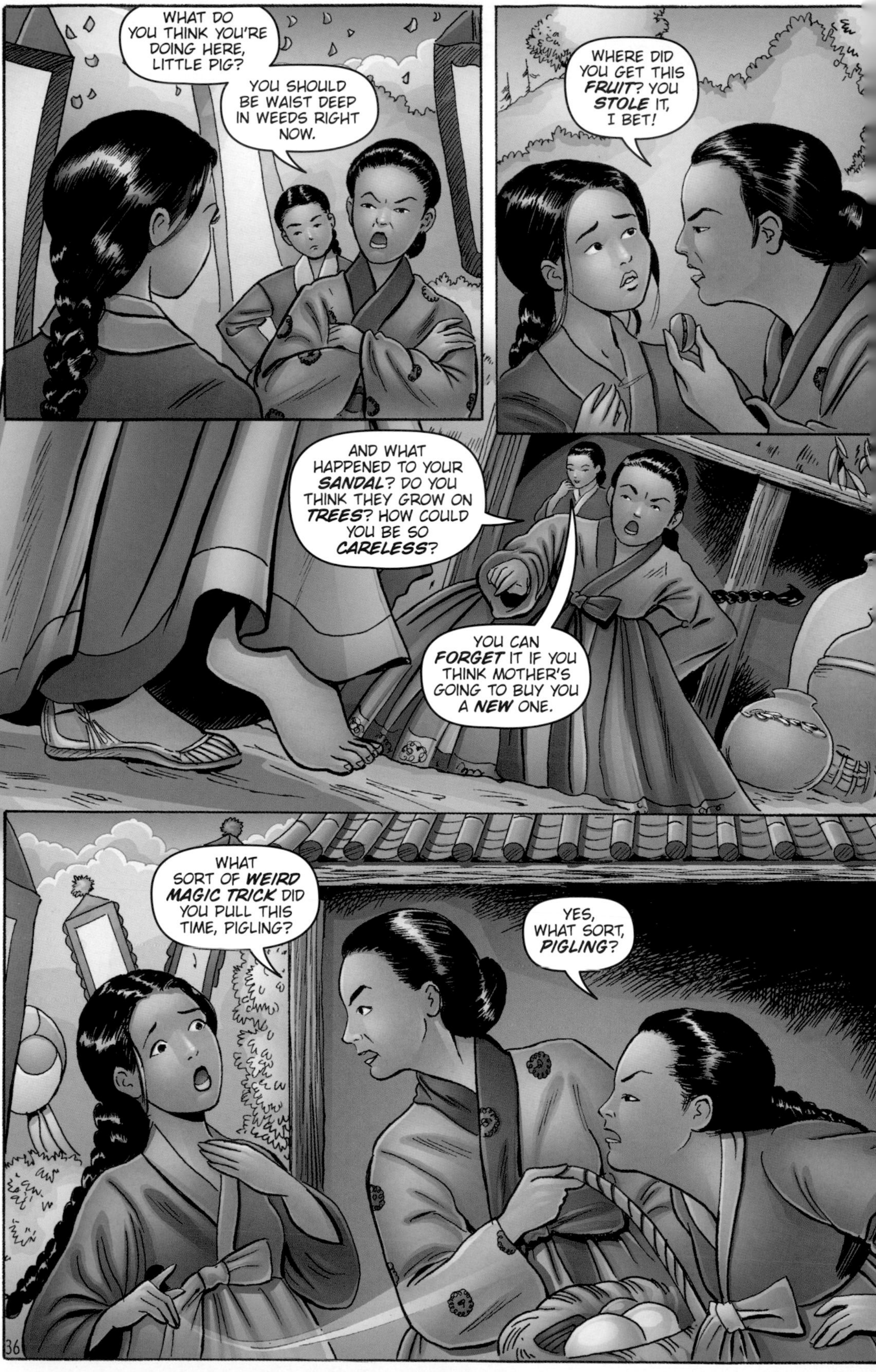
WHAT DO YOU THINK YOU'RE DOING HERE, LITTLE PIG?
YOU SHOULD BE WAIST DEEP IN WEEDS RIGHT NOW.
WHERE DID YOU GET THIS FRUIT? YOU STOLE IT, I BET!
AND WHAT HAPPENED TO YOUR SANDAL? DO YOU THINK THEY GROW ON TREES? HOW COULD YOU BE SO CARELESS?
YOU CAN FORGET IT IF YOU THINK MOTHER'S GOING TO BUY YOU A NEW ONE.
WHAT SORT OF WEIRD MAGIC TRICK DID YOU PULL THIS TIME, PIGLING?
YES, WHAT SORT, PIGLING?

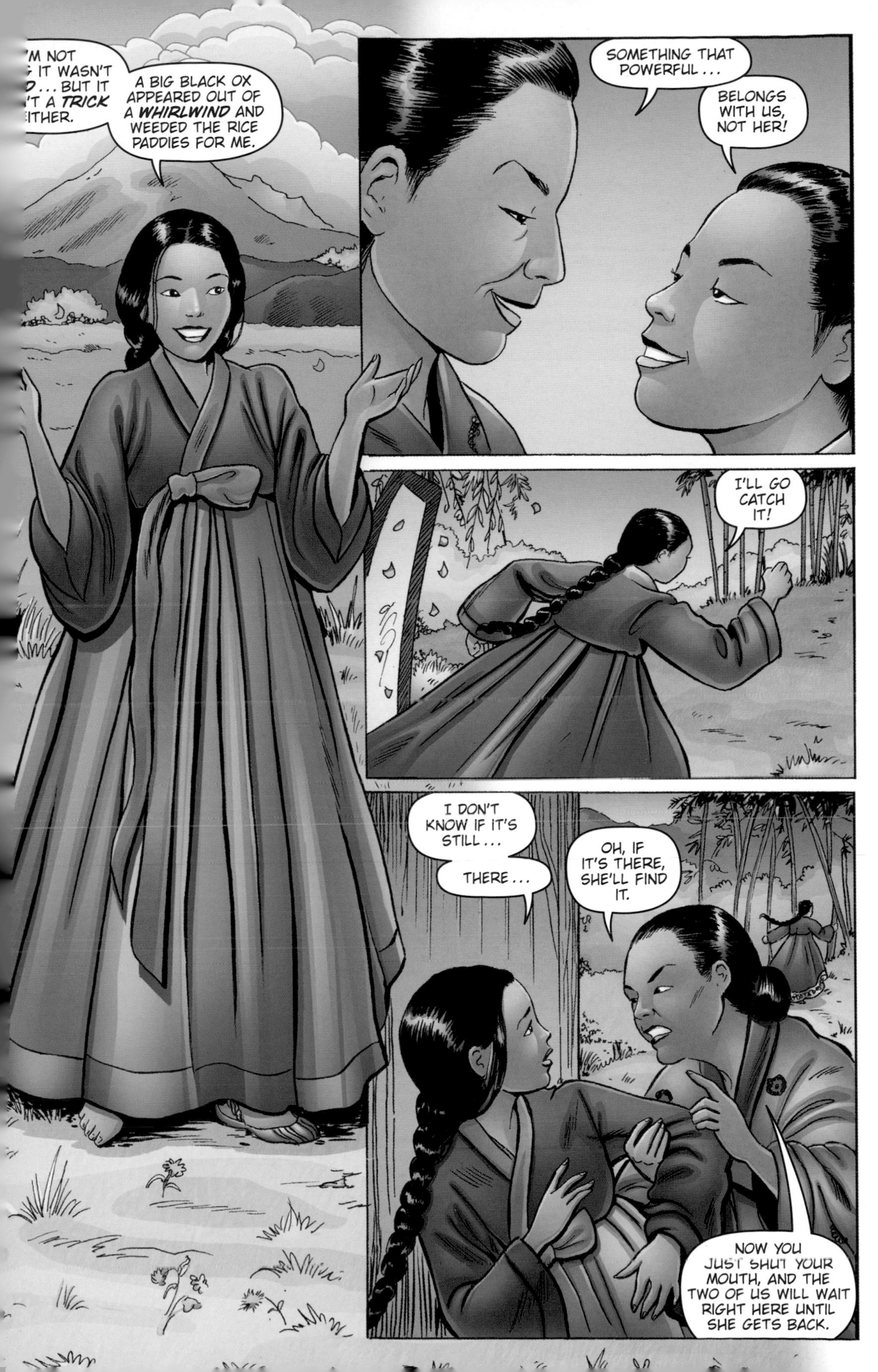
'M NOT IT WASN'T ... BUT IT 'T A TRICK EITHER.
A BIG BLACK OX APPEARED OUT OF A WHIRLWIND AND WEEDED THE RICE PADDIES FOR ME.
SOMETHING THAT POWERFUL ...
BELONGS WITH US, NOT HER!
I'LL GO CATCH IT!
I DON'T KNOW IF IT'S STILL ...
THERE ...
OH, IF IT'S THERE, SHE'LL FIND IT.
NOW YOU JUST SHUT YOUR MOUTH, AND THE TWO OF US WILL WAIT RIGHT HERE UNTIL SHE GETS BACK.

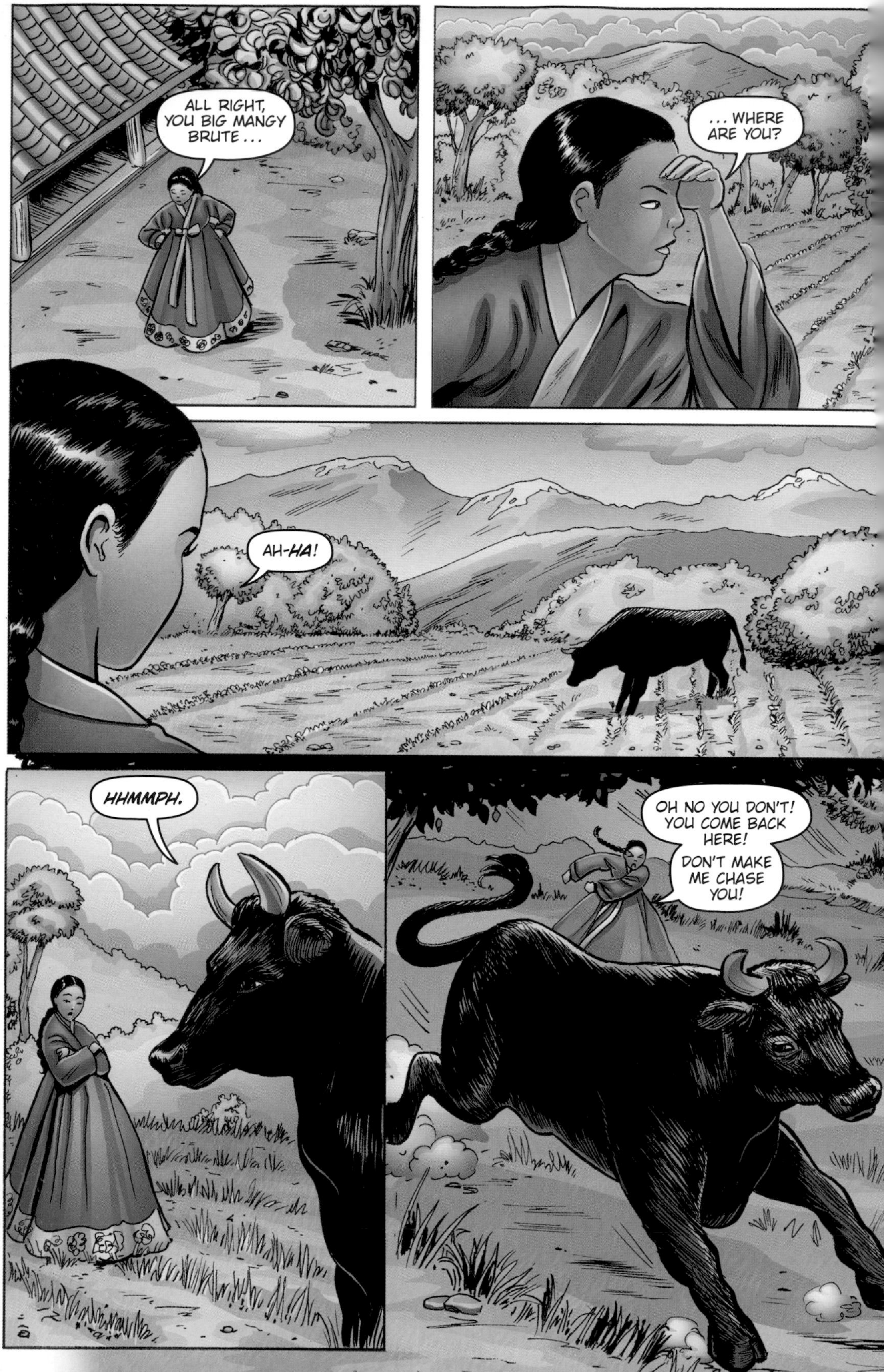
ALL RIGHT, YOU BIG MANGY BRUTE . . .
. . . WHERE ARE YOU?
AH-*HA!*
HHMMPH.
OH NO YOU DON'T! YOU COME BACK HERE!
DON'T MAKE ME CHASE YOU!

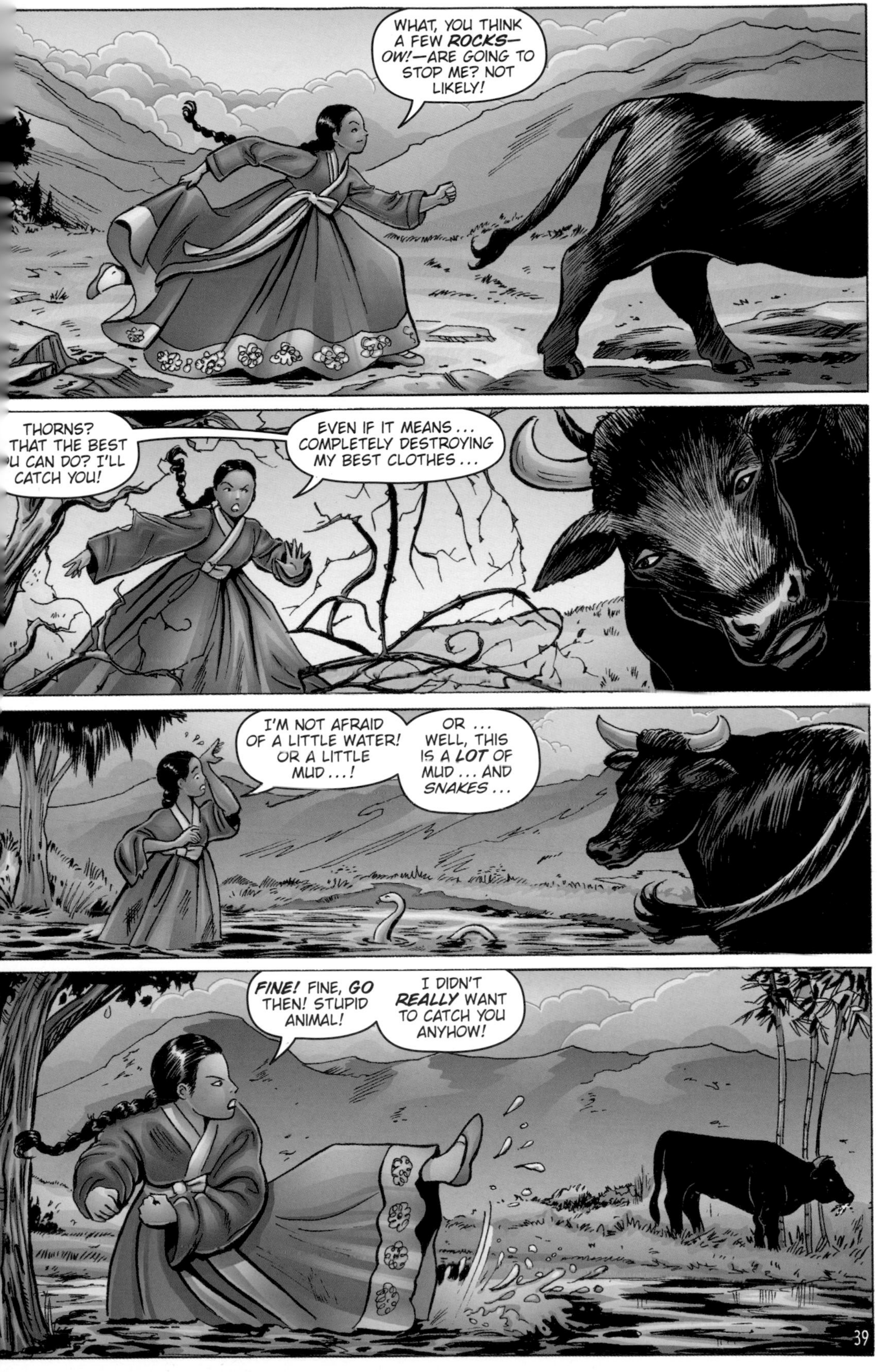
WHAT, YOU THINK A FEW ROCKS— OW!—ARE GOING TO STOP ME? NOT LIKELY!
THORNS? THAT THE BEST U CAN DO? I'LL CATCH YOU!
EVEN IF IT MEANS . . . COMPLETELY DESTROYING MY BEST CLOTHES . . .
I'M NOT AFRAID OF A LITTLE WATER! OR A LITTLE MUD . . . !
OR . . . WELL, THIS IS A LOT OF MUD . . . AND SNAKES . . .
FINE! FINE, GO THEN! STUPID ANIMAL!
I DIDN'T REALLY WANT TO CATCH YOU ANYHOW!

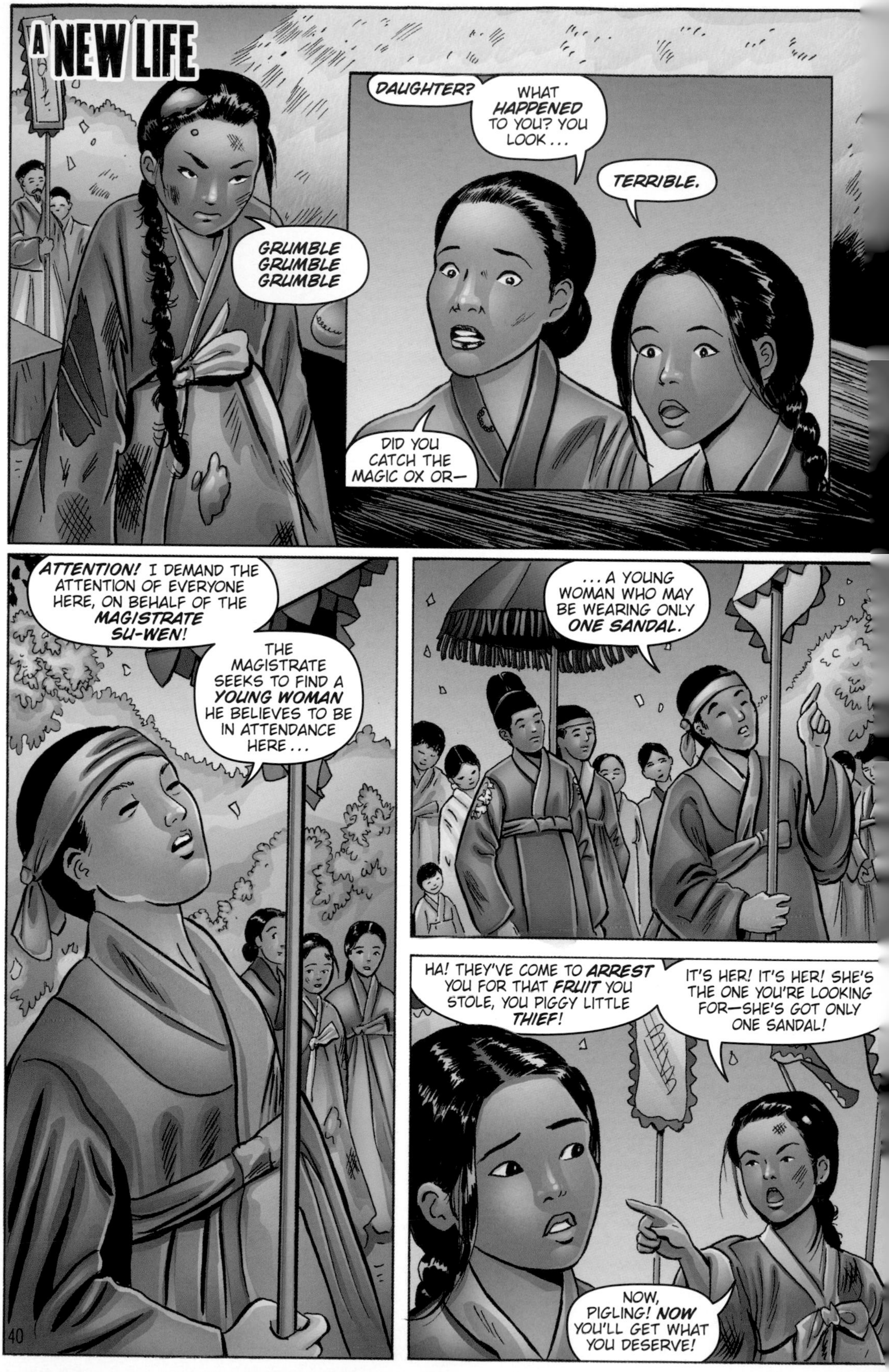
A NEW LIFE
GRUMBLE GRUMBLE GRUMBLE
DAUGHTER?
WHAT HAPPENED TO YOU? YOU LOOK . . .
TERRIBLE.
DID YOU CATCH THE MAGIC OX OR—
ATTENTION! I DEMAND THE ATTENTION OF EVERYONE HERE, ON BEHALF OF THE MAGISTRATE SU-WEN!
THE MAGISTRATE SEEKS TO FIND A YOUNG WOMAN HE BELIEVES TO BE IN ATTENDANCE HERE . . .
. . . A YOUNG WOMAN WHO MAY BE WEARING ONLY ONE SANDAL.
HA! THEY'VE COME TO ARREST YOU FOR THAT FRUIT YOU STOLE, YOU PIGGY LITTLE THIEF!
IT'S HER! IT'S HER! SHE'S THE ONE YOU'RE LOOKING FOR—SHE'S GOT ONLY ONE SANDAL!
NOW, PIGLING! NOW YOU'LL GET WHAT YOU DESERVE!

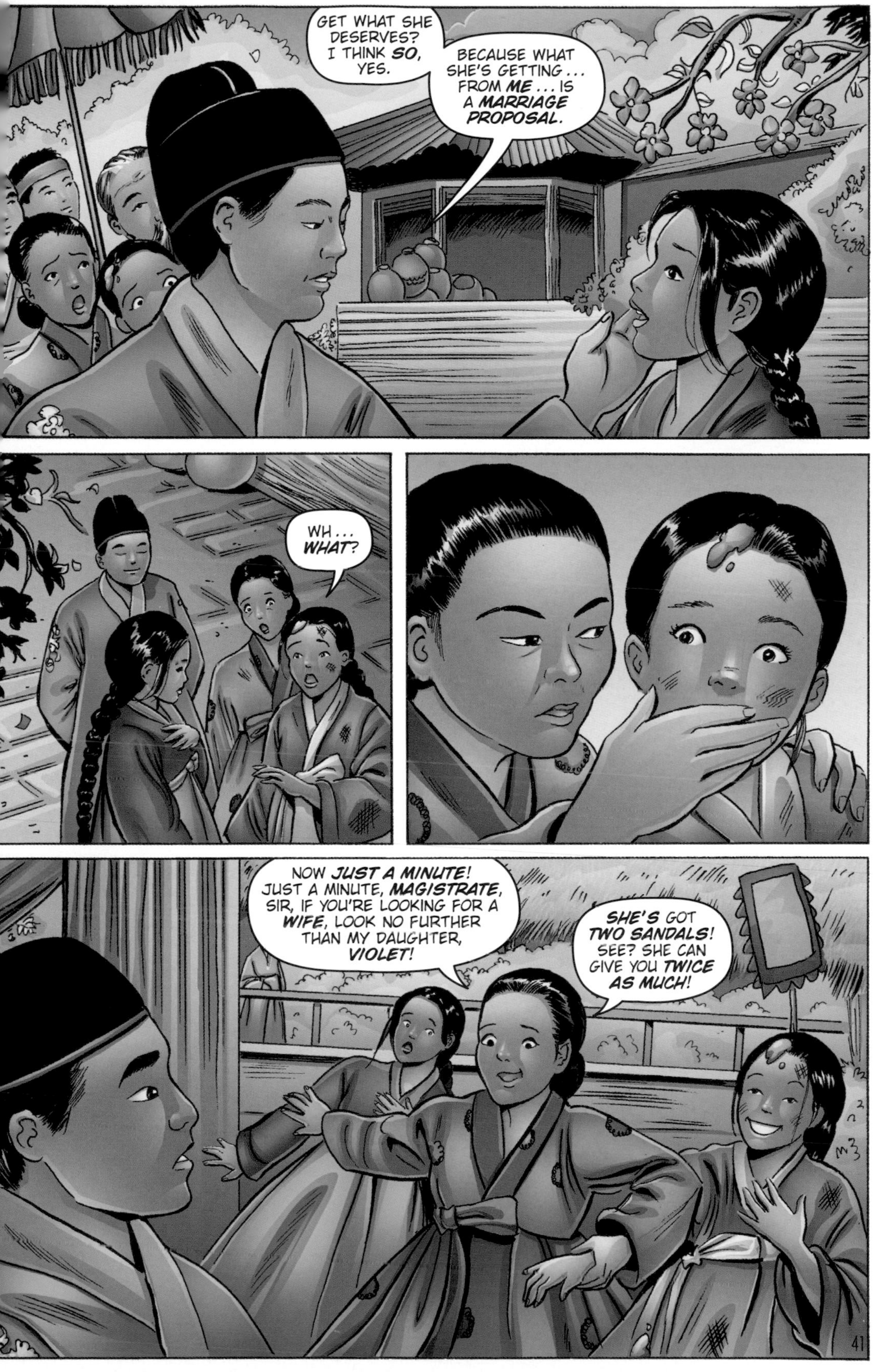
GET WHAT SHE DESERVES? I THINK SO, YES.
BECAUSE WHAT SHE'S GETTING . . . FROM ME . . . IS A MARRIAGE PROPOSAL.
WH . . . WHAT?
NOW JUST A MINUTE! JUST A MINUTE, MAGISTRATE, SIR, IF YOU'RE LOOKING FOR A WIFE, LOOK NO FURTHER THAN MY DAUGHTER, VIOLET!
SHE'S GOT TWO SANDALS! SEE? SHE CAN GIVE YOU TWICE AS MUCH!

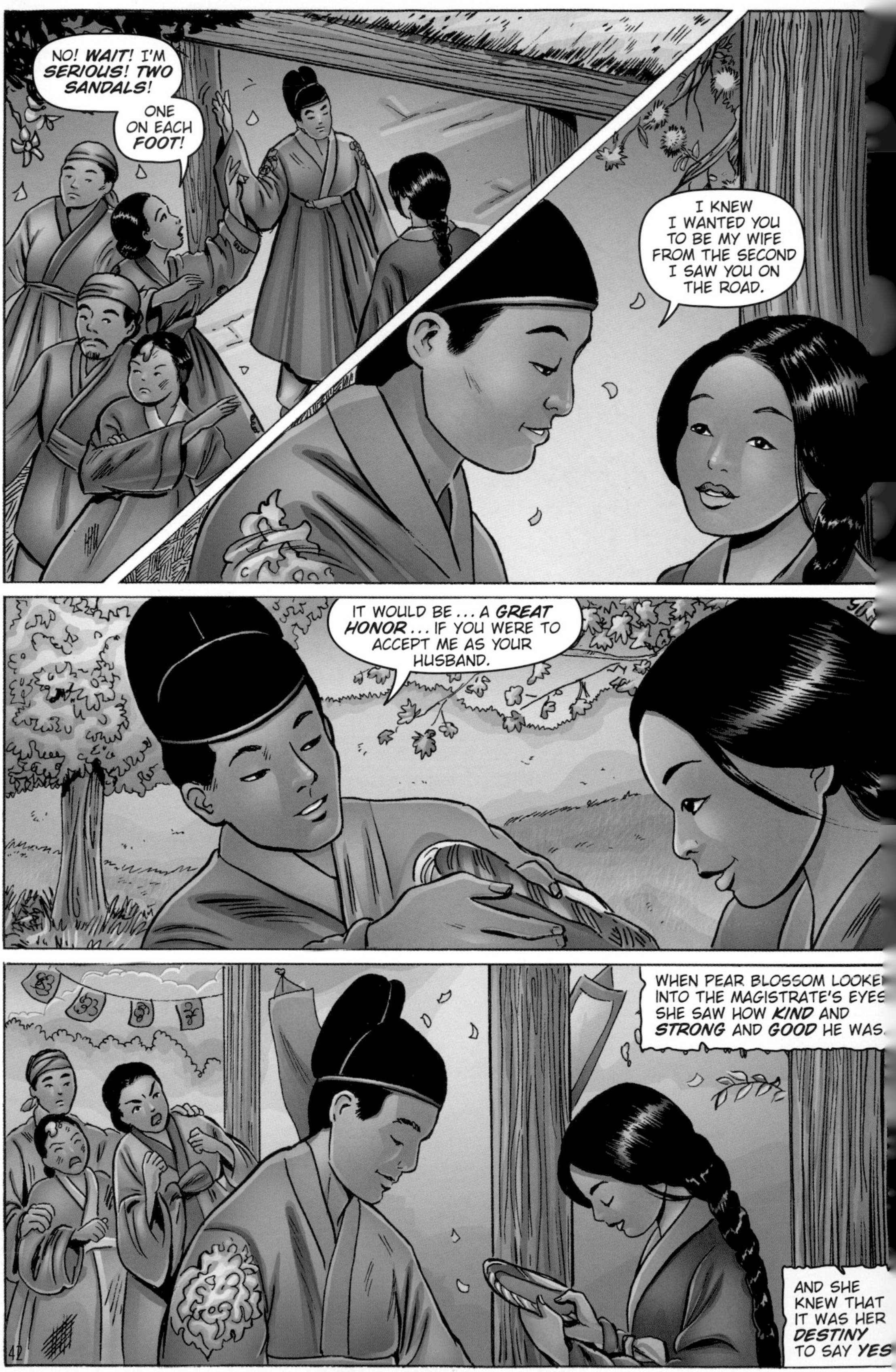

NO! WAIT! I'M SERIOUS! TWO SANDALS!
ONE ON EACH FOOT!
I KNEW I WANTED YOU TO BE MY WIFE FROM THE SECOND I SAW YOU ON THE ROAD.
IT WOULD BE . . . A GREAT HONOR . . . IF YOU WERE TO ACCEPT ME AS YOUR HUSBAND.
WHEN PEAR BLOSSOM LOOKE[D] INTO THE MAGISTRATE'S EYES SHE SAW HOW KIND AND STRONG AND GOOD HE WAS.
AND SHE KNEW THAT IT WAS HER DESTINY TO SAY YES

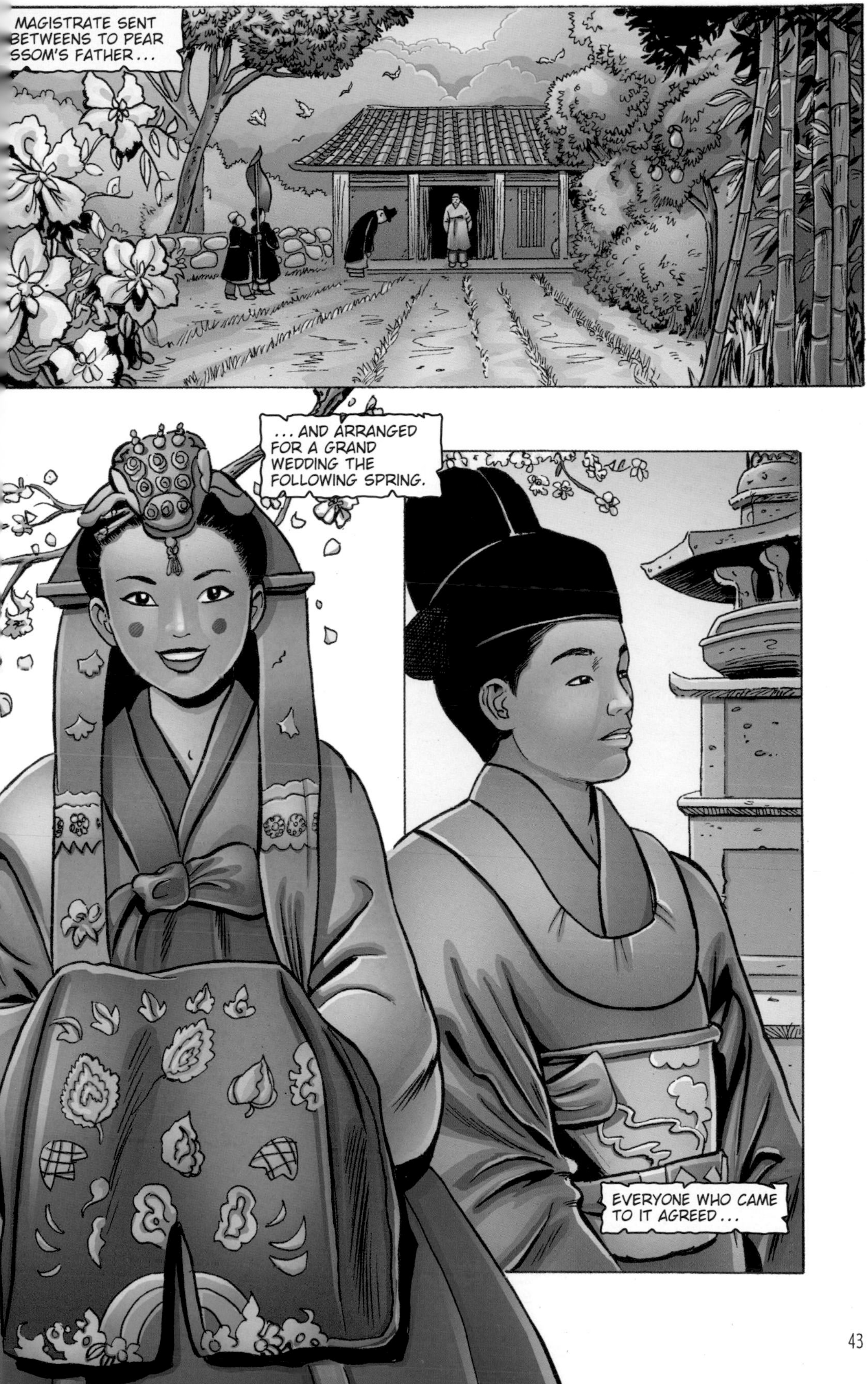
MAGISTRATE SENT
BETWEENS TO PEAR
SSOM'S FATHER...
...AND ARRANGED FOR A GRAND WEDDING THE FOLLOWING SPRING.
EVERYONE WHO CAME TO IT AGREED...

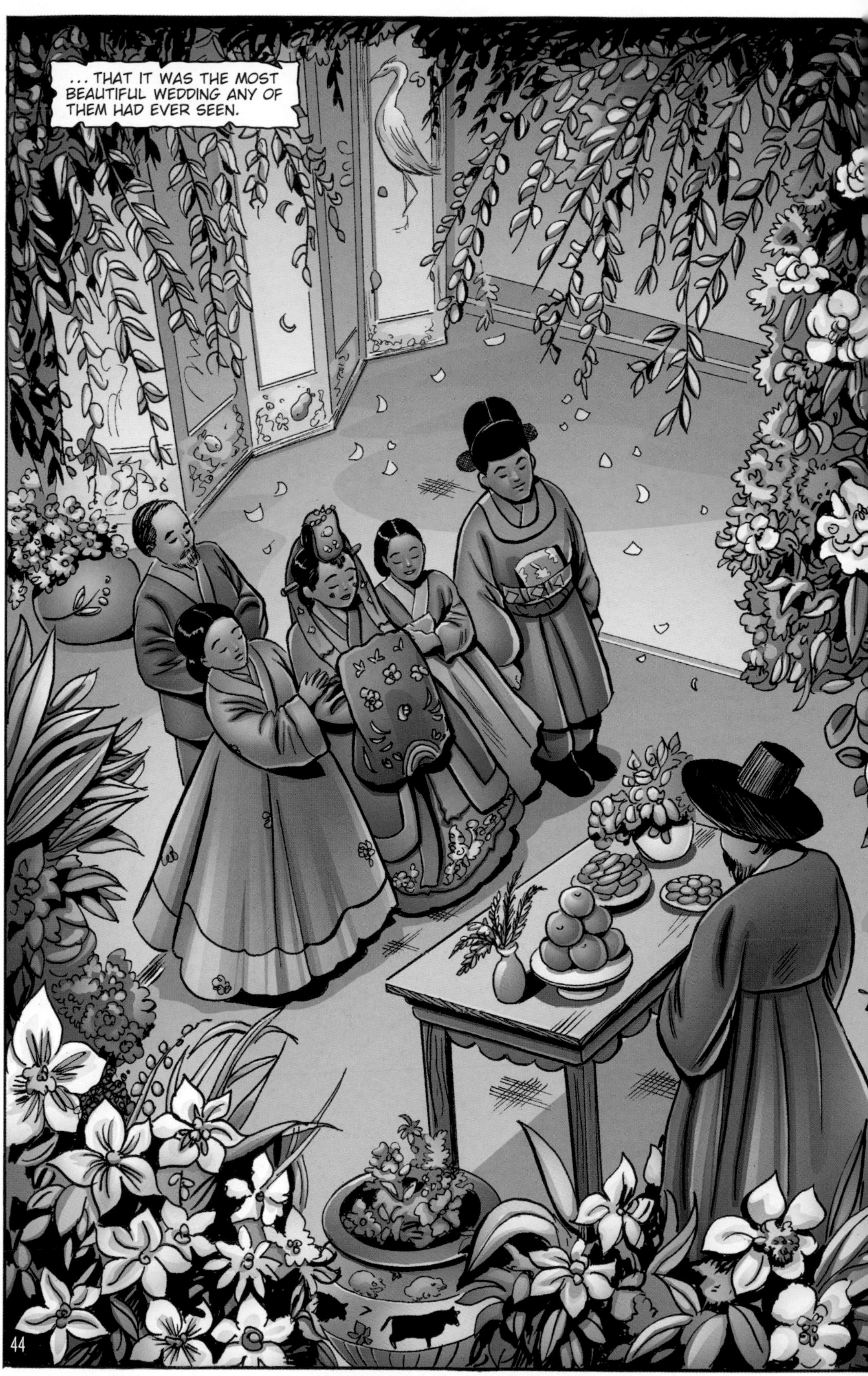
. . . THAT IT WAS THE MOST BEAUTIFUL WEDDING ANY OF THEM HAD EVER SEEN.

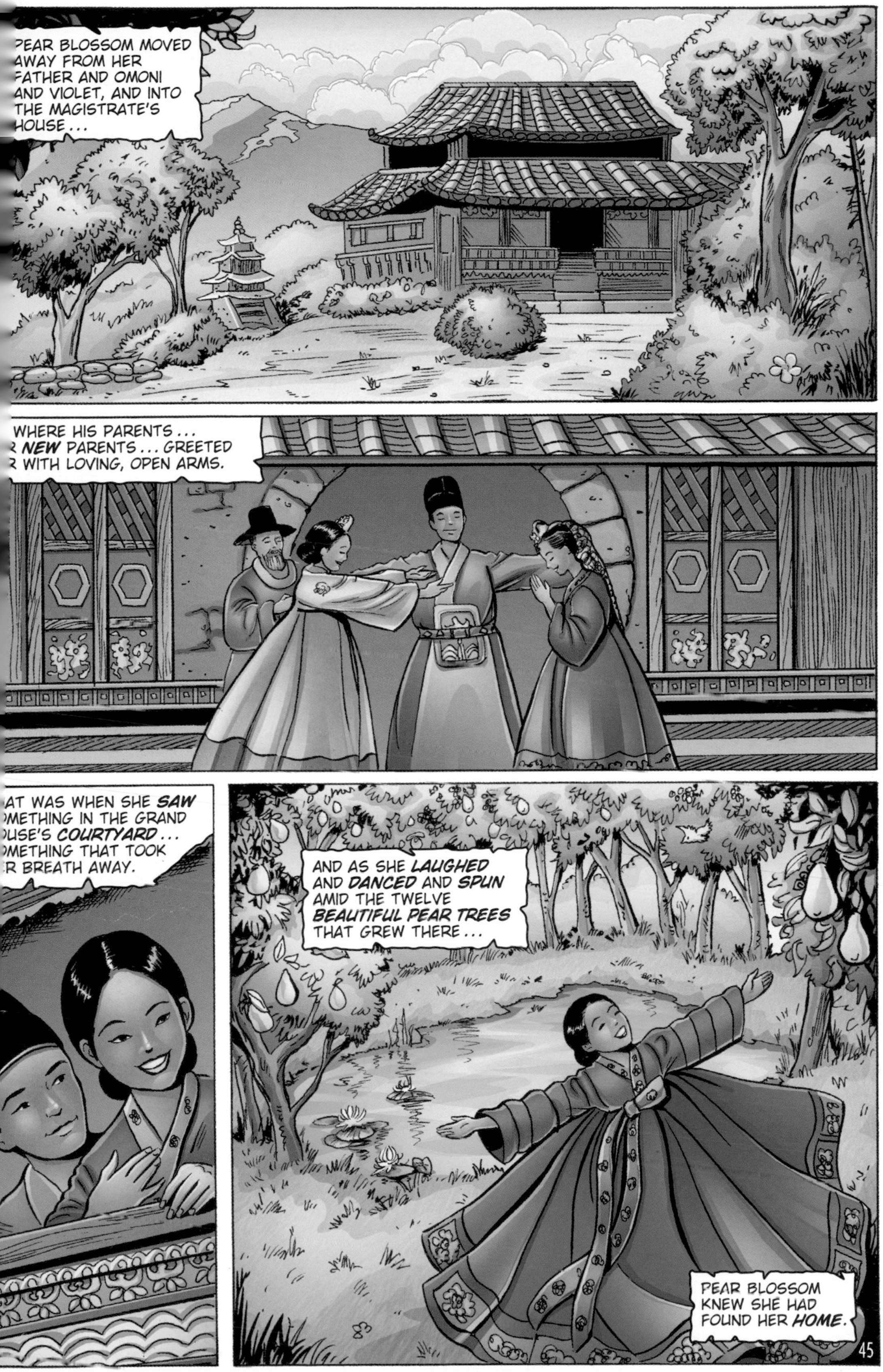
EAR BLOSSOM MOVED AWAY FROM HER FATHER AND OMONI AND VIOLET, AND INTO THE MAGISTRATE'S HOUSE...
WHERE HIS PARENTS... R NEW PARENTS... GREETED R WITH LOVING, OPEN ARMS.
AT WAS WHEN SHE SAW OMETHING IN THE GRAND OUSE'S COURTYARD... OMETHING THAT TOOK R BREATH AWAY.
AND AS SHE LAUGHED AND DANCED AND SPUN AMID THE TWELVE BEAUTIFUL PEAR TREES THAT GREW THERE...
PEAR BLOSSOM KNEW SHE HAD FOUND HER HOME.

GLOSSARY AND PRONUNCIATION GUIDE

GO-BETWEEN: a person who helps people to communicate or to reach an agreement. Pear Blossom's future husband sent go-betweens to Pear Blossom's father to reach an agreement about the couple's marriage.

HULL: to separate the outer covering from a seed

MAGISTRATE (*maj*-uh-strate): an official who rules over a land or a nation

MATCHMAKER: a person who brings unmarried people together to arrange a marriage

NOBLEMAN: a man who is born to an important family or who holds an important position

OMONI (aw-*maw*-nee): the Korean word for "mother"

OX: a large mammal related to the cow

PADDY: wet land where rice grows

PROPOSAL: a suggestion or an offer. *Proposal* often refers to a marriage offer.

TORNADO: a strong windstorm accompanied by a funnel-shaped cloud

WIDOW: a woman whose husband has died

original pencil sketch from page 26

FURTHER READING AND WEBSITES

Climo, Shirley. *The Korean Cinderella*. New York: HarperCollins Publishers, 1993. Climo's picture-book version of the Korean Cinderella story features detailed paintings and Korean words and expressions.

Fleischman, Paul. *Glass Slipper, Gold Sandal: A Worldwide Cinderella*. New York: Henry Holt, 2007. This enchanting title marries many different traditions. It interweaves seventeen Cinderella stories into one multicultural fairy tale.

Holman, Sheri. *Sondok: Princess of the Moon and Stars*. New York: Scholastic, 2002. Read the fictional diary of Princess Sondok, the girl who became queen of Silla, South Korea, in A.D. 632.

Hidden Korea: Culture
http://www.pbs.org/hiddenkorea/
Learn interesting facts about Korean culture at this website from PBS.

Time for Kids: South Korea
http://www.timeforkids.com/TFK/hh/goplaces/main/0,20344,927166,00.html
Explore South Korea at this site, which includes a sightseeing guide, a fun quiz, and e-cards you can send to your friends.

CREATING *PIGLING: A CINDERELLA STORY*

To create *Pigling: A Cinderella Story*, author Dan Jolley relied on various versions of the story, including William Elliot Griffis's *Pigling and Her Proud Sister* as it appears in Olive Beaupré Miller's *Through Fairy Halls*. Jolley shaped his adaptation of the tale in consultation with Minsook Kim, Ph.D., of the University of California, Berkeley. Artist Anne Timmons consulted various historical sources while completing artwork for the book. She worked closely with Kim to ensure accuracy in her depictions of Korean customs and culture.

INDEX

ABOUT THE AUTHOR AND THE ARTIST

DAN JOLLEY began his writing career in the early nineties. His limited series *Obergeist* was voted Best Horror Comic of 2001 by *Wizard Magazine*, and his DC Comics project *JSA: The Unholy Three* received an Eisner Award nomination (the comics industry's highest honor) for Best Limited Series of 2003. In recent years, he has cowritten two novels based on licensed properties: *Star Trek SCE: Some Assembly Required* and *Vengeance*, from the television series *Angel*. May 2007 saw the debut of Jolley's first solo novel series, an original young adult sci-fi espionage story called *Alex Unlimited*, published by a joint venture of TokyoPop and HarperCollins. Jolley lives in Cary, North Carolina, where he works as a computer game designer for Icarus Studios.

ANNE TIMMONS was born in Portland, Oregon, and received her Bachelor of Fine Arts degree from Oregon State University. In addition to her collaboration with Trina Robbins on the Lulu Award-winning *GoGirl!*, Timmons's work includes the Eisner-nominated *Dignifying Science* and the comic-book version of *Star Trek: Deep Space Nine*. She has illustrated and painted covers for children's books and provided interior and cover art for regional and national magazines, including *Wired*, *Portland Review*, and *Comic Book Artist*. Timmons's art also appears in the anthology *9-11: Artists Respond* and is now part of the Prints and Photographs collection at the Library of Congress. Timmons and Robbins recently collaborated on a graphic novel adaptation of Jane Austen's *Northanger Abbey*, which came out in 2007. Samples of Timmons's art can be seen at http://www.annetimmons.com.

$8.95 U.S.A.

FROM A LIFE FILLED WITH HARDSHIP . . .
. . . COMES AN UNMATCHED BEAUTY DESTINED FOR A FAIRY-TALE ENDING.

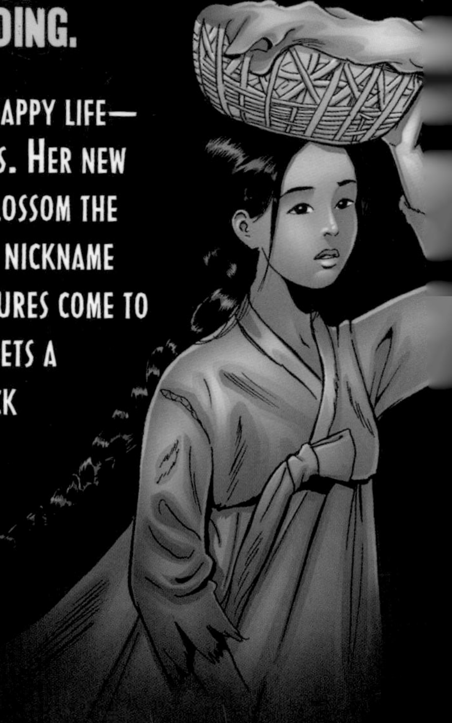

Pear Blossom, a young Korean girl, leads a happy life—until her mother dies and her father remarries. Her new wicked stepmother and stepsister make Pear Blossom the victim of their cruelty. They even give her the nickname Pigling, or little pig. But soon, magical creatures come to Pear Blossom´s aid—and one day, the girl meets a handsome magistrate. Will Pear Blossom´s luck change for the better? Or is she destined to suffer at her stepfamily´s hands forever?

GRAPHIC MYTHS AND LEGENDS TITLES:

- ALI BABA: FOOLING THE FORTY THIEVES
- AMATERASU: RETURN OF THE SUN
- ARTHUR & LANCELOT: THE FIGHT FOR CAMELOT
- ATALANTA: THE RACE AGAINST DESTINY
- BEOWULF: MONSTER SLAYER
- DEMETER & PERSEPHONE: SPRING HELD HOSTAGE
- GUAN YU: BLOOD BROTHERS TO THE END
- HERCULES: THE TWELVE LABORS
- THE HERO TWINS: AGAINST THE LORDS OF DEATH
- ISIS & OSIRIS: TO THE ENDS OF THE EARTH
- JASON: QUEST FOR THE GOLDEN FLEECE
- KING ARTHUR: EXCALIBUR UNSHEATHED
- MARWE: INTO THE LAND OF THE DEAD
- ODYSSEUS: ESCAPING POSEIDON´S CURSE
- PERSEUS: THE HUNT FOR MEDUSA´S HEAD
- PIGLING: A CINDERELLA STORY
- PSYCHE & EROS: THE LADY AND THE MONSTER
- ROBIN HOOD: OUTLAW OF SHERWOOD FOREST
- SINBAD: SAILING INTO PERIL
- THE SMOKING MOUNTAIN: THE STORY OF POPOCATÉPETL AND IZTACCÍHUATL
- SUNJATA: WARRIOR KING OF MALI
- THESEUS: BATTLING THE MINOTAUR
- THOR & LOKI: IN THE LAND OF GIANTS
- TRISTAN & ISOLDE: THE WARRIOR AND THE PRINCESS
- THE TROJAN HORSE: THE FALL OF TROY
- WILLIAM TELL: ONE AGAINST AN EMPIRE
- YU THE GREAT: CONQUERING THE FLOOD

GRAPHIC UNIVERSE™
A DIVISION OF
LERNER PUBLISHING GROUP
WWW.LERNERBOOKS.COM

ISBN 978-1-58013-825-3
50895
9 781580 138253